THE SPARE

THE SPARE

----- Part II -----

Marsha May Fairchild Sumpter

ARPress
ILLUMINATING IDEAS
EMPOWERING VOICES

ARPress
45 Dan Road Suite 5
Canton MA 02021

Hotline: 1(888) 821-0229
Fax: 1(508) 545-7580

Ordering Information:

Quantity sales. Special discounts are available on quantity purchases by corporations, associations, and others. For details, contact the publisher at the address above.

Printed in the United States of America.

ISBN-13:   Softcover   979-8-89330-310-0
             eBook   979-8-89330-311-7

Library of Congress Control Number: 2024900957

To Bill and our family

CONTENTS

PREFACE

The writing of this book and the first one is just to give a glimpse into the life on the farm when I was growing up, and carry you through the trials and tribulations encountered along the way.

In many ways, my story is very insignificant because I realize there are many people out there that encountered way more difficulties and survived them. Each and every person has a story to tell, and it is unfortunate they don't write about it and let others know what it is like to be a survivor.

Times repeat themselves, and it is with intestinal fortitude that people can move on and make the best of what is happening around them. It seems you can always see others that are in worse shape than you are. Time is nature's way of preventing everything from happening at once.

Thank you for taking the time to read these books, and may you feel the urge to sit down and write your own story for at least your family to know you better.

INTRODUCTION

Marriage—a simple word to pronounce, but it holds so many unknowns. It is the union of two people with totally different backgrounds, upbringing, and expectations. If taken seriously, it is a commitment to work as a team in a relationship and see it through.

The standard marriage vows go something like this, "Do you take this woman to be your lawfully wedded wife, to have and to hold, in sickness and in health, until death do you part?" And the other part is for the wife to repeat.

It's brief and to the point, but it is a union that joins a couple. Bill came from a broken home, an only child raised in Arkansas. He was raised, in part, by his grandparents Mamie and Boon Sumpter. His mother was born to Mamie, when she was married to James Riley, along with two more sisters and two brothers. When James passed away, Mamie married Boon Sumpter, who had three children of his own—NW and two daughters. Their two kids, Virgie Riley and NW (Narvel Wesley) Sumpter—stepbrother and stepsister—found themselves pregnant. They married, and from that marriage, a baby girl was born, who did not survive, and Billy Ray was born September 12, 1940. Soon they discovered that they had drifted apart. NW enlisted in the military and eventually was assigned to a post in Rapid City, at the Rapid City Army Air Base, which was a training base for the B-17 Flying Fortress.

In 1952, the base was renamed to be Ellsworth Air Force Base. NW met and married his second wife, Beatrice (Cashman) Sumpter. In 1958, Billy Ray graduated from Wynne, Arkansas, High School and made the move to South Dakota to live and work for his dad. Living in the north, he was soon known as Bill rather than Billy Ray.

My folks struggled through many trials in their married life but stuck it out to the end, "until death do us part." After sixty-four years of marriage, my dad, Wayne Fairchild, passed away at the age of ninety-one, in 2002, and my mother, Ruth Fairchild, at the age of eighty-eight in 2006. Mom said divorce never entered her head, but murder did quite often.

Here we were, embarking on the complex union of two very different people from two different cultures, in the hope that this marriage would succeed.

In the day, it was called a shotgun wedding, where it depicts the father holding a gun to make the man marry his daughter. In this case, it was our decision to be married, probably against the wishes of my dad. We soon discovered that opposites attract.

THE NEWS

We were pregnant! There was no test you could buy at the local store; you just let Mother Nature let you know such things. You also can't be just a little bit pregnant. Now the time of reckoning for our careless behavior had come. Bill and I drove to Philip to break the news to my folks. It didn't go over too well.

What were we thinking? Here we were, me just seventeen and Bill twenty, and I was still in school! The main comment was, "You made your bed, now lie in it." Which meant in other words, "You're on your own." The plan was to get married. We next went to his dad and stepmom to let them know the thought process us kids were going through. With that behind us, we next needed to figure out what all it would take to get married. We didn't have any friends with experience in such a situation, so we just muddled along on our own. We knew you needed blood work in order to be married, thinking there was a three-day waiting period on that. We rolled up our sleeves at the Bennett Clarkson Hospital and got the blood drawn, and the technician told us there was no three-day waiting; the results would be done in about an hour. It was a Monday, February 6, 1961, and I had skipped school, and Bill had taken off from work; so with that information, we got busy. Bill had a nice pair of dress pants that had a tear in them and needed cleaning; they went to the one-hour dry cleaning in Baken Park, where they were mended and cleaned.

We needed a place to live! Well, we had heard about some little cabins that rented for $40 a month at Black Hawk, so we headed there and rented a cabin. Bill had the $40 to cover that. As the door to this little cabin opened, we were greeted with a musty unused smell. It was partially furnished. A free-standing wardrobe was pushed up against the wall next to the doorway. As you walked in, to the right was a small table with two chairs, and pushed into a small space next to the kitchen wall was a small refrigerator with a little freezer in it. The bed consumed the better part of this room. You could get around both sides of the bed; unless someone was sitting at the table, then it was a problem. In the kitchen was a small stove. There was a single sink beside that with minimal counter space and some shelves for dishes and pots and pans on the far wall. The bathroom, which was off the kitchen, had a stool and shower and was so small it was hard to shut the door; you had to plan ahead or just leave it open. The good news was the price included water, heat, and sewer. What more could we ask for?

Okay, things were falling into place. The next order of business was to get a license and find a justice of the peace to get married by.

ELOPE

We went to the Cashman Café, where Bill's stepmother, Bea, worked with her sister-in-law Arzie Cashman. We visited with Arzie and told her how things were going. We did need to have a couple stand up with us. It was a Monday, and it just so happened that the barber, who didn't work on Monday but had a shop there at the café, was there, and he said he and his wife would be happy to stand up with us. For some unexplained reason, we decided to elope to Sturgis, about forty miles from Rapid. We got to the courthouse and bought the license, then were advised that we would have to have a telegram from parents before any ceremony could be performed because we were both underage. What a difference a year would have made because the legal age to be married then was eighteen for a girl and twenty-one for the guy. There wasn't anything like the phones of today, so we used a pay phone to place a collect call to my mom and ask her to wire a telegram to the Meade County Courthouse, giving her consent for us to get married. Another long-distance collect call to Bea with the same request. Mom had to make quite a drive to get to Philip to send the telegram, and it was rather late arriving, making us nervous it wasn't coming. When the telegrams arrived, and all things were in order, the justice of the peace came and performed the ceremony. He had been out fishing; it was such a warm and beautiful day. We returned to Rapid and dropped off our witnesses.

Even though the little cabin was furnished, that still left us with no bedding, dishes, or silverware and such for setting up housekeeping. There weren't any secondhand stores like there are now, so we went begging. We got to Bill's folks' place that evening and asked if they had any of the items we needed.

Bea wanted to see the marriage license before handing over anything but finally rustled up some bedding, two plates, two forks, two knives, two spoons, and two cups for us. That was how we started our married life together.

COOKING

Bill's Aunt Arzie came by one day and showed me how to make gravy so it wouldn't be lumpy and gave me other cooking hints since she was a cook at the Cashman Café and had lots of good tips. I discovered that Bill would eat anything that was put on a plate and shoved in front of him, even if he wouldn't, by choice, put certain food on his own plate. So I fixed his plate and served him, and he would eat it all. He did like ketchup, and I kidded that I could feed him dog or cat food and ketchup, and he'd wolf it all down. Just to let you know, I never did do that to him.

FRIENDS

One couple we liked was Dawn and Ivan Ramisch. I ran into Dawn one day, shortly after Bill and I were married, and she followed me out to the cabin. I told her we'd gotten married. It wasn't long after that she and Ivan got married. We attended the wedding, in a church officiated by a minister. We were too young to be witnesses for them, so they had another couple do that. We remained friends and enjoyed one another's company. Again, they were in the same boat we were—very poor.

RETURN

Dad had said that if we got married, my car—that hot 1955 Mercury that got the attention of this guy I married—had to come home. He and Mom arrived at the cabin, and in return for the car, they gave us a sewing machine and a small nine-inch black-and-white TV that we could, with rabbit ears, pick up two channels from Rapid City. The little cabin was about twelve miles from Rapid. That left us with one car, which we seemed to take in stride. We would get up early, and I would drop him off at his folks so he could go to work for his dad, and I would go to school.

SCHOOL

I managed to get my studies done and advised the principal of my marriage and pending baby. They were very accommodating and, because of the many steps to the various classes, asked if I wanted to change that around. Exercise is good for a person, and because I was young, the answer was no. In some schools, the students had to take correspondence courses so as not to influence other students or bring embarrassment to the school. I was thankful the Rapid City High School didn't do that. I graduated in June 1961.

DOG

For some unknown reason, we thought we had to have a dog! What were we thinking? We could hardly afford our own food, and of course, there was the expense of cigarettes and beer for Bill, as well as what we ate. But at any rate, we went to the nearest animal pound to see about getting a dog.

We looked at all the cute little puppies, and there in a cage was an older Boston bulldog. The fee to adopt the dog was $20, which we didn't have. Would they take payments? We put $2 down, and home came this little bulldog. The habit he had that sent him to the pound in the first place was he would tear up things in the house. Well, our house wasn't very big and didn't have a lot of things to tear up, so we figured we'd get along quite well. I can't even remember the dog's name, but he was very protective of me, and if Bill would pretend to hit me, the dog would fight him, never tearing any skin but definitely barked, growled, and snapped to give him the idea that wasn't acceptable. The bad thing was we would play that way on the bed, and when it was time for Bill to go to bed, the dog wasn't too sure about him being there.

We discovered if he was left in the house, and we didn't get home at the usual time, then something would get torn up; it happened to be a pillowcase once. After that, I would take him with me to school on nice days, and he would wait in the car; I would let him out when I had breaks and be sure he had food and water. Once, though, Bill and his friends came and got the car and lost the dog. I think we had him paid for by then, and it may have been intentional.

Because construction work with Butch, a.k.a. NW (Bill's dad), was sporadic, Bill took a job working for Mayflower Movers out of Rapid City. He had a buddy that worked for them and got him the job. They moved a lot of Ellsworth Air Force Base folks, and one day, here came

Bill and a doghouse and a dog that must have been part Great Dane. He was lanky and stood about hip-high on me. He had big paws that looked like he was going to grow into them. This mutt liked to sleep in the bed with us, but he was so big that if he stretched out, we both about fell out of bed. We had to keep him outside when we were both gone, but he was a Houdini of escape and then would try to find us. One time, I was driving down Main Street in Rapid—you have to remember, this is over twelve miles from where we lived—when I spotted him come running toward the car, I opened the door, and in he flew. He heard that car through all the traffic. He always knew when Bill was about a half-mile from home and would stand by the door. He got loose one too many times and tried to follow the car. We never found him that time.

LAUNDRY

We had no way to wash clothes except to use a Laundromat and that took money. Usually I would put the clothes in a clothes basket and carry them along until I scraped together enough coins to run a load of clothes, then bring them back to the cabin and hang them up. We didn't have a lot of clothes, so it got to be a problem at times. Once Mom and Dad came by to visit as I was getting out of school, and they asked why the clothes were in the back seat. I had to tell them we didn't have the money to get them washed; it brought tears from me to have to confess that to them.

I don't recall if they gave me any money to ease the situation. The Laundromat had a large sink, but there was no stopper to hold the water. If I got really desperate for certain clothes, I would stuff a clothing article in the drain and scrub the clothes, wring them out, and take them home to dry on the line. Not the best way to wash clothes, and my fingers sometimes would bleed from the scrubbing, but it worked.

To the Rescue

Mom and Dad—probably with Mom pushing—decided that we needed to have better living conditions before the baby arrived. They found a very nice used Magnolia trailer home, 8'×40". It got set up in the same trailer court where we had rented the cabin. They paid for the trailer using money Dad said was from selling cows I had (I didn't know I had any cows to sell!). We moved into this glorious little trailer. The kitchen had a wall-mounted GE refrigerator; two doors were refrigerator, and one was a freezer. Best idea I'd ever seen. It was above the double sink, which was a corner sink, then the stove, and still room for a table and chairs. Storm windows were stored in a slot beneath the refrigerator, which divided the living room from the kitchen. The living room was large enough for a couch and chair, end table, and a cradle. A middle aisle went between two twin beds that each had a footlocker-type storage at the end. Then the bathroom with a tub, toilet and a sink, and a clothes hamper built in, and finally into the main bedroom with a built-in chest of drawers and small closets on each side of that. It was compact but a mansion to us. We gave up the dog idea and ended up with a kitten—a black long-haired kitten that grew into a beautiful cat. A visiting German shepherd would come over, and I didn't need to dust after he had been there. He was so big that when he stuck his nose out to be petted by Bill, sitting across from the door, his tail would clear anything off the end table, and when he turned around to leave, it was the same. Thus dusting was done!

ABANDONED

Well, maybe abandoned is a rather harsh way to put it, but it seemed that was the case. Here I was, very much pregnant, and Bill said, "Let's go visit this couple. The guy was friends with Bill. We arrived at their little rental house along Omaha Street in Rapid City. They were in the same boat we were—very poor; I don't think they even had a car. At any rate, as the visit wore on, Bill and the fellow decided to leave in our car and go somewhere; we weren't invited to go along nor were we told where or how long they would be gone.

It was now night, and still no Bill nor our car. I was getting plumb mad about the entire situation, and about eleven thirty at night, I decided I'd had enough. I was tired, and the other gal was too, so I took off walking back to Black Hawk. I had a church key bottle opener in my pocket for protection, and I was stomping mad. I took off to Main Street to have the benefit of streetlights in my favor, and off I went. Only one drunk approached me as I walked past the bars of downtown, and I was so mad that when I responded to his advances, he backed off.

I had walked about two miles and was just getting to the outskirts of Rapid by the Meadowood Bowling Alley when a police car pulled up beside me. The officer was pleasant and wondered if I was going to work. I replied no. Then he wondered if I was just getting off work; again, no. I told him the whole story and that I was walking to Black Hawk because that blankety-blank husband of mine left me stranded in town. The kind officer gave me a lift home. We were still living in the little cabin at the time. The vow we took when we got married was "until death do us part," and right then, murder was on my mind! The excuse given when he got home fell on deaf ears, but we stuck it out. No murder that night.

HOW BROKE?

There came a knock on the cabin door one evening while we were watching that little black-and-white TV. It was a salesman. He had a deal we couldn't live without. He was selling portraits that would be taken at JCPenney's in downtown Rapid. The cost was only $1 for the 8"×11.5" picture. He would set up the time and take care of everything for us. Between us, we didn't have even a dollar. As he visited, he noticed the cigarettes on the wardrobe. Cigarettes were $.33 a pack at the time. He said he would take three packs of cigarettes and put in the dollar, and we could have the picture taken. What a deal. Bill agreed to give up those three pack of cigarettes. At the appointed time, we cleaned up and kept the appointment for the picture.

That was in March of 1961. I could still fit in my graduation dress, and Bill cleaned up good, too. He wore his hair in a flattop DA. The picture was in black and white, and I had a colorizing kit, so using that, I added the color.

DANCE AND DOCTOR

On July 15, I turned eighteen and was approximately seven and a half months pregnant. The next weekend, we decided to go visit the folks. There was a lot of activity going on at the farm/ranch, and on Saturday night, there was even a dance at Cottonwood. Bill and I, along with other friends, went to the dance. It seemed that drinking took up a lot of the evening for the men. I enjoyed dancing with Bill and other fellows I knew. It was an enjoyable time visiting, good music, and as always, a lunch served around midnight.

The next day, what was happening? I was losing water and experiencing some pain. We went to Rapid, and I checked in to the St. John's Hospital. I didn't have a doctor, hadn't seen one during the entire pregnancy because we had no insurance, and it would cost to keep appointments with a doctor.

The loss of water was a clue that the baby was getting close to delivery. At first, the attending doctor tried to stop the process, and I was kept in the hospital. I was up walking around and was so little with baby that some said those women that already had their baby were bigger.

After attempts to stop the birth, nature took its course, and a dry birth happened. The doctor had to make the opening bigger, then stitch it back up after delivery.

We really weren't prepared for a baby. My cousin from Wisconsin, Barbara Vesaas, was visiting, and she suggested calling this new little girl Shelley, which suited both of us. We knew the middle name would be May, since that was a name handed down from many generations, that the firstborn girl would have the middle name of May. My Aunt Edna—firstborn—got the middle name of May, and my mom didn't have a middle name, and when she married, she kept her maiden name of Sherwood. The May name goes clear back to Dorothy May, who came over on the *Mayflower* in 1620 and was the middle name of Louisa May Alcott, also a relative. Shelley May Sumpter sounded good to both Bill and me, so that is what went on the birth certificate. Shelley was born July 25, 1961, and weighed in at 4 lbs., 10 oz.

When I arrived at the hospital, I was barefooted and wearing hand-me-down maternity clothes. The nuns at the hospital questioned me if I had any shoes.

Well, I rarely wore shoes in the summer months, so the answer was we'd try to find a pair. I had a good-sized foot, usually taking a size 10. Bill rounded up a few things and brought them to the hospital, including a pair of shoes.

BABY SHELLEY

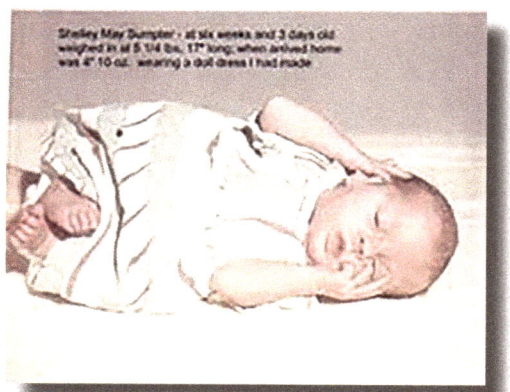

Shelley May Sumpter - at six weeks, and 3 days old weighed in at 5 1/4 lbs, 17" long; when arrived home was 4" 10 oz. wearing a doll dress I had made

Probably due to the fact we didn't have any kind of insurance and looked pretty much like hillbillies, Shelley and I were released from the hospital before she gained any weight at all. She was wrinkled and jaundiced, and a doll dress I'd made many years ago fit her perfectly.

There was no money for bottles or formula, so it was breastfeeding. At the hospital, they were prepared to give me something to dry up the milk, but that was changed.

I certainly wasn't a milk cow. In order to get her to drink, I had to use a nipple shield, and probably because of that, she was colicky. Babies didn't come with a book in that day and age. It seemed like she was always crying or on the nipple. Then I experienced something I'd never had before—menstrual cramps, which were worse than labor pains by far, just a few days after I got home. I did call the doctor's office and discovered there was a remedy for that, so we managed to get some medicine over the counter, and that eased the situation.

In order to have a car, I would take Bill to work, or a coworker would pick him up. I still carried around clothes that needed washing and did all the shopping, trying to stretch what little money we had to cover all the essentials. I had a small handheld adding mechanism; it was metal, and it had a small metal pen that you would input the cost of things, and it added them up, which helped me keep track of what cash I had and items in the shopping cart.

In Philip, all the neighbors held a baby shower for us, and we received cloth diapers, baby clothes, and necessities, which were much appreciated. We brought the antique cradle back with us, and it was put to good use as a daybed, and then we would put it on the bunk to keep her safe and closer to our bedroom.

That kitten we had grew up, and folks were afraid for us to have a cat in the house—the old wives' tale was that it would take the baby's breath away. Jinx was a loving cat, and when Shelley was out of the cradle, he played with her rattles. Jinx was bigger than Shelley.

It seemed that sleep was something I never got. She cried a lot, and I would lie on the other bunk bed and breastfeed her and fall asleep in the process.

We didn't have a car seat or bed, so one of Bill's beer boxes rode on the passenger seat with Shelley in it, and if she got too fussy, I would pull over, put her on a nipple and drape a receiving blanket over my shoulder and her, and drive to where I was going. It didn't matter if I was shopping, walking down the street, or whatever; it seemed she was always hungry. Bea said she was starving to death because I didn't have enough milk. We did get a couple of bottles, and she had water and juice and even started eating baby cereal and baby food early.

One day, another salesman came by with the fabulous Stroll-O-Chair. It was a combination of everything you needed for a baby to a

growing little one. All you needed to do was put the wheels in the trunk, wedge the baby buggy between the front and back seat, and you had a baby bed; and when you got to where you were going, it became a baby buggy. It consisted of five items that interchanged: the car seat and table became a high chair, a stroller, table and chair, and a rocking chair. The baby bed also could become a rocker. The cost of this combination was $400. Boy, that was a bank buster, but the salesman was a minister in Sturgis, and he would be willing to set up a payment schedule for us. After talking to Bill about it, we made a trip to Sturgis, and we became the proud owners of the Stroll-O-Chair (which I still have in our shop today, but we would be charged with child abuse if we used it for any of our great-grandchildren).

Once Bill was going to be helpful, there were clothes that needed to be hung out in a basket in the car, and he had the car. He went to the Laundromat and, without looking into the basket, dumped it in the dryer and then went away for a while. Well, unbeknownst to him, there were a couple of jars of baby food that had fallen into that basket. They broke in the dryer and made a total mess of all the clothes and the dryer. It was a sad deal.

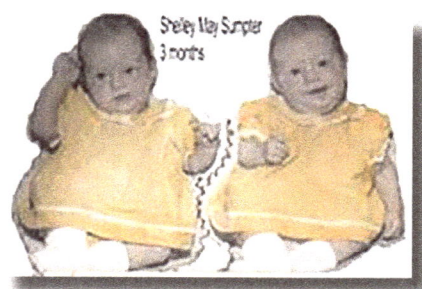

Shelley May Sumpter
3 months

Another time, when I was getting groceries, Shelley had a blowout of diarrhea, and everything was totally a mess. I was at Baken Park at the time, and the only place that had baby clothes was Haggerty's. They were an expensive store, much more expensive than I could afford, but Mr. Haggerty saw the predicament I was in and gave me a discount on the cutest corduroy outfit. It was such high quality that not only did Shelley wear it until she outgrew it, but second daughter, Sandra, did, too.

No Insurance/Big Wind

Here it was, December, I had our little trailer decorated with a half tree that hung on the wall that was silver tinsel, had managed to either make Christmas presents, baked some things, sewed some with the sewing machine wedding gift, and purchased a very few. We were struggling to keep ahead of bills. We had parking rent to pay each month, gas to get to and from places, even though gas was only $.19 with $.04 tax, making it $.23 a gallon; it still was a major expenditure, plus laundry and groceries.

When the folks got the trailer for us, nobody thought about insurance on it. After all, it only cost $2,300 for that awesome little trailer. We certainly couldn't afford any insurance on top of everything else, so we were uninsured against anything.

It was just a few days before Christmas 1961, when the terrible wind came up, the temperature was around ten below zero, and a light snow on the ground.

Bill, Shelley, and I had been visiting at friends, and Bill had been enjoying his beer. When we got back to the trailer, it was leaning to the east, and the wind would blow hard out of the northwest, and it would lean more to the east, then rock back as the wind let up. It seemed that some of the blocks on the east side had broken. The head of our bed was on the east side of the bedroom, and before we went to bed, I made him turn it around. I said if I was going to die that night, it would be feetfirst!

It didn't take Bill long to fall asleep, Shelley was asleep in the crib on the west bunk bed, and I was wide awake, scared to death every time the trailer would get hit with the wind. It would rise up, then settle back down, except for one time, the wind got a second breath, and over went the trailer! The furnace had blown out earlier, so fire wasn't a threat, but cold was. I had slept with my clothes on because I was so nervous; when everything turned over, Bill had to find his clothes. Our bed slid to the end of the room, dumping us out of it. I climbed up to the door of the bathroom and promptly fell into the toilet. The sliding door to the little bedroom where Shelley was, jammed; I had to climb back out of the bathroom, and as luck would have it, both of the outside doors were on the topside now. I pushed open the outside bedroom door, ran along the trailer—barefooted—opened the other door, and dropped into the living room. Even though the other sliding door was closed, I was able to open it and get to Shelley.

As luck would have it, when the trailer went on its side, she was thrown to the other bunk, and the crib turned upside down over her; she was unharmed, just scared. By now Bill had gotten his wits about him and clothes on and was able to open the door I couldn't budge. We got out and went to the neighbors to the east; their trailer was anchored down, and they still had heat and electricity. Bill was holding Shelley and bouncing her on his knee.

I said, "She's not crying. You can quit bouncing her."

He said his knees were shaking so bad he couldn't stop them. I went back in our overturned trailer with a flashlight and found Jinx, the cat, and rescued him. We were homeless just before Christmas.

We gathered up enough things to get by that night and headed off to Rapid, to his folks' place. We didn't have a telephone, so it was a surprise when we showed up there well after midnight. In the trailer court, there were four other trailers that got flipped at the same time. Had it not been for some steps on the east side of our trailer, I think it would have been all right, but they punched into the kitchen when it went over.

We called Mom and Dad the next morning to tell them what happened, and there were folks from Rapid City that sold trailers that came around and made offers on getting folks into another trailer. We went with Green Star Mobile Homes; they had a Champion mobile home with a living room slide and would make a trade, pull our trailer beside theirs so we could move things easy, and set up on a lot of our choice and would arrange payments.

We found some land for sale in Rapid Valley, Pioneer Drive, and the owner, Don Payne, would make it into a trailer court with five spots for the price quoted. We settled on that, and when it was ready, the trailer we bought was moved into the spot by the road, leaving us four possible rentals, which may help pay expenses down the road. We even had our own water source.

Haste makes waste, and we discovered that we probably should have shopped a little harder for a trailer. The Champion had water leaks where the slide out was, discovered this on the very first rain. It was poorly made, and when the wind blew, it would make the living room wall move in several inches. The good news—it had three bedrooms and a washing machine in the little bathroom, so no more trips to the Laundromat. I had a clothesline set up in the backyard, so that was wonderful.

Because we weren't too smart about things, it seemed that every winter, we had frozen water pipes, even though we had it wrapped with a heat tape. I spent a considerable amount of time in the cold of winter under that trailer with a torch thawing the line. I often thought that it would be to our benefit if it caught fire; all we had of any value was a little bigger TV, plus a few clothes.

We lived there from early in 1962 until 1964. We did rent three spots out, but that was a major headache, we soon discovered. They were late with rent, and if anything went wrong—like their waterlines freezing—they pestered us.

JOBS

The good news about the move to Rapid Valley was that Bill was much closer to work. He was still working for his dad and Dutch Muckler, running a Caterpillar and driving truck. They had the bid to provide shale to the cement plant. There was still way too much alcohol consumed at his work and after work.

Shelley was little, but I felt I needed a job to help make ends meet. I answered an ad in the newspaper for a bus driver. You have to remember, I was only eighteen, but I had been raised on the farm/ranch and could drive trucks. I showed up at the interview, as did a middle-aged man. The position was a part-time job—in the morning and evening, picking up kids and dropping them off. The fellow that did the interview and driving test was set on intimidating me.

He gave me a pretty good driving test, and I passed that. He cussed and swore, thinking that would be a problem for me; however, if you ever worked sheep or cattle, you know about every cuss word there is. He finally turned his attention to the other fellow, asking him what he did that he was able to take on driving part-time. The man said he was pastor at the Episcopalian Church. Boy, that made the interviewer feel real small, considering the language he'd been using. We both got hired. I was driving a seventy-three-passenger bus. We both were assigned to picking up kids at Ellsworth Air Force Base. If we had a bad day or such, I would stop by his bus and say, "Boy, that's about enough to make a preacher cuss," which would bring a big smile and promise of a better day tomorrow. This was in 1962, and there was no age limit on bus drivers nor was there really a test, background check, or any of the things now required.

The base kids were well behaved, and some would even pack some extra goodies in their lunch just for the bus driver. They never made a mess in the bus, and threw their wrappers and things in a waste paper box I kept by the door. I had one Lutheran boy, and the rest were Catholic. On days the Catholic school was off, I still had to make the run in that big bus to pick up that one little boy.

There was another lady bus driver, and she had a run from Rapid City to Farmingdale and Caputa to the East; it was close to one hundred miles each day. On the Ellsworth run, it was all elementary kids, but the Farmingdale/Caputa run was high school and junior high kids, and they had this gal completely buffaloed. She quit, and the boss offered me that run. The good news was I could keep the bus right at our house and start from there rather than driving across Rapid City to get it. I jumped at this opportunity. The bus company also didn't mind if Shelley was a passenger, so I saved a little on babysitting that way.

Since the kids had gotten away with tormenting the other lady bus driver until she quit, I think they were planning to do the same with me. The first day on the morning run, the kids left the bus a terrible mess with paper, candy wrappers, and whatever. It was the bus driver's responsibility to keep the bus clean, and each night before you quit, you had to go through and sweep it up.

That night, I put brooms and dustpans on the bus, and when we were about ten miles from anywhere I parked the bus, put on the hazard lights, and advised the kids they could either clean up the floor of all the things thrown there or walk home. There was a bit of a standoff, but finally, the worst offenders started cleaning up the mess. I kept a waste paper box by the front of the bus, and from then on, things were thrown where they belonged.

The first ones to line up to get on the bus would look to see if Shelley was awake; if she was sleeping, they passed the word along to the others, and they very quietly got on the bus and got seated so as not to disturb her. If she fussed, one or more of the students would take her out of her seat and play with her.

Kids will be kids, and one night, after we were on the route toward home, I noticed in the mirrors a car following us. It was tailgating the bus. What I didn't know was some of the kids on the bus had gotten the ones in the car all heated up, and were also in the back of the bus making obscene gestures to those in the car. You have to remember,

these are all teenagers. Well, when I stopped to let one of the kids off at their approach, I went back to those in the car and advised them that the girl walking home from there was going to call the police and report they were tailgating the bus, so if they didn't want to get into more trouble than they were already in, they better stop. That ended that problem.

You always have favorites, it seems, and I had one boy that was a real nice kid. He was helpful and respectful. One stormy night, as I was picking up the kids, the headlights and windshield had accumulated a lot of snow before the kids got in. I asked this boy to jump out and clean away the snow, and to my surprise, he refused. Instead, he offered to open and close the door as students came to get on. Well, that was all right with me, and I got out and cleared away the snow, but while I was outside the bus, he put it in gear and moved it ahead a little. When I got back on the bus, I made him get out and go call his parents to come and get him. You didn't move the bus under any circumstances, and he had to be punished. The next morning, when I stopped at his approach to get him, there sat his dad with him, in the car. The boy had vowed he was never going to ride the bus again because I had embarrassed him. However, as soon as I swung the door open and smiled, he relented and climbed in, never causing a problem after that. In fact, the other boys gained a new respect for this bus driver as well.

BABY NUMBER 2

The route I had driving bus was a little too rough when I was expecting our second child, so I had to quit. Bill and I enjoyed bowling, and the folks at the bowling alley needed a short-order cook, would I like the job. Well, why not? It couldn't be too difficult to do, so I accepted. I had found a wonderful babysitter, Mrs. Paulson, who lived in the valley and not too far away from us, so that was a blessing. I worked as the cook at the counter during the day. When I got too big and uncomfortable to do that, I worked in their nursery they had so women could bowl during the day and not worry about babysitters.

August 14, 1963, was when our second daughter, Sandra Raye, was born. She was a beautiful plump baby, 9 lbs., 10 oz., all pink and nothing like our firstborn, Shelley. She was also breastfed, and unlike when I was feeding Shelley, she didn't nurse that often, and that was a problem. I had to wear milk shields to catch the milk that would secrete before she was ready to nurse.

With two children at home and nursing, I then took on the job of taking care of two children in the neighborhood, Curt and Paula Christensen, whose folks lived just across the street from our trailer. We still didn't have but one car, and Bill used that most of the time for work. I would bundle up the four kids, and we would have a wagon train to walk and pay the electric bill or get exercise

or visit the neighbors. In this picture, I was also taking care of another little girl. There was a delivery truck from Gate City Creamery that came down our street, and because going to the grocery store was a problem, I started getting products off the truck. They carried milk, butter, cottage cheese, ice cream, and some meat products, etc. I took the delivery for about a month, and when we got the bill, it was a shock—we couldn't afford that service. I got the bill paid and, from then on, shopped by reading the newspaper we got from the neighbors, making a list of what was on sale and what we needed. That cut our grocery bill in half or better, and Bill had to make sure I had the car to do the shopping.

One time, when Bill went grocery shopping with me, and I was using my little metal calculator to keep track of how much I was spending, he added extra things to the cart. When we got to checkout, we had more items than I had money. He was so embarrassed because I had to have the clerk take things off to match the money available. After that, he didn't go shopping with me. Not until way later in life.

READ THE SIGNS

After we got married, I soon found out that Bill was a man of few words.

How can you find those things out when you talk a lot, and you two seem to kiss a lot! At any rate, when we first married, he was content to spend time with me after his work and my school. However, I think as the baby grew, and I got bigger, he thought he needed more space to himself.

He would gather things he needed, like cigarettes, and quietly leave the house, jump in the car, and be gone to spend time with whomever he planned to spend time with, leaving me home alone with no car. I made friends in the trailer court but was totally upset with being left behind and no explanation of what or where he was going.

After Shelley was born, he would do the same thing; only I soon learned to read the signs when he was getting ready to fly the coop, and had a bag all set out to grab, along with Shelley, and jump in the car before he could get there. Thus reading the signs was important. He still didn't say too much but accepted that we were along for the ride, wherever it took us.

BLEAK LONELY NIGHTS

Well, Bill figured out how to keep me from jumping in the car to go with; he just never came home to give me the opportunity! There is a fine line between love and hate, and I fell from one to the other quite easily. Supper would be prepared, and he didn't come to eat it with the family. The drinking at work and then stopping after work at the local bar was not something I bargained on.

As he was celebrating his twenty-first birthday, he was so carelessly driving that I made him take Shelley and me home. He then proceeded to take off again to finish his celebration. Well, lucky for him, when a police officer pulled him over, he was lenient and just told him to go home. Bill's excuse for digging out at a stop sign was that the motor mount must be broken and had to have stuck the gas pedal. That little fiasco could have cost us a lot of money we didn't have.

The more Bill spent time drinking, the more discouraged I got, also the angrier as well. When he did finally show up at home, I didn't waste much time in telling him what I thought. Why did I let him cause me so much pain? At one time, I even considered the thought of death over living like that, my own.

Long-distance phone calls were another expense, but I even called his mother in Arkansas and told her what a no-good son she had raised. Boy, was I mad about the entire situation, and Bill was never there to tell. His dad was instrumental in helping him lead such a careless life because that is what he did. His stepmom, Bea, understood some of my frustration. Bill's stepdad, Erby, was also a drinker.

One time, Bill came home with Roy Dean Liebig with him, thinking that would calm me down. I had the revolver sitting on the counter, with bird shot in it, and proceeded to take a couple of shots out the door, and the fire that leaped from the muzzle of the gun and the loud report was enough to scare Roy Dean, and he tried to crawl under the car. After the dust settled, Roy Dean asked me to take him home. Another time, Bill made friends with a fellow that was from the Philip area, Gale White. His parents were Blake and Mildred White. I remember the first time I met him, Mom and Dad were going to visit the Whites and Gale. I thought Gale was a girl and was happy to go along on the ride, only to be disheartened to find out it was another boy, as if I didn't have enough of them around. Mildred became the Pennington County Treasurer when they moved to the Rapid City area. At any rate, that night, Bill and Gale showed up, and I had had enough; I had thrown Bill's clothes out the door, into the snowbank. Here they came, and I relented and opened the locked door and let them in. Lesson learned, I had to retrieve all the things thrown out in the yard; Bill didn't care enough about them to worry about it.

I can't remember who Bill went hunting with, another drinking buddy; at any rate, they were night hunting, and he brought home a couple of rabbits for supper. One way to get the wife to clean them was to start plucking the fur off and having it float all around the house. I had to take charge and skin them proper and take the guts out. Then it was feast time on those rabbits. All you had to do was prepare them like chicken.

It was during one of these long dark nights that I decided it was time to make a change. If in fact, Bill was going to continue to do as he was, then I needed to figure out a way to be a single mom if it came to that. I needed some education!

More School

I checked into the National College of Business for a way to get a better-paying job. They had a nine-month course called Stenographic and Office Machines, and it was something I could accomplish and be able to afford, I figured. School had been hard for me before, and it was no easy task with two little girls.

Mrs. Paulson was the best babysitter and only lived a little ways from us. The course taught speed writing, typing, grooming, office machines, and penmanship. Since I had good penmanship, I challenged that course, not wanting to waste time on something I already know. They did let me do a writing test, sent it into the Palmer Method Company, and I was excused from that course.

When I started school, Bill was better at typing than I was. You had to type so many words without errors on a manual typewriter. I spent many hours practicing typing and speed writing in order to graduate. To help pay for the babysitter and school, we took in girls attending school as boarders. We had a set of bunk beds for the girls' bedroom, but I needed another set. I made a bargain with a lady to sell her the full-size bed for $20, which she gave me a check for. I then went to a secondhand store and bought a set of bunk beds for $40, giving them a check.

Well, to make a long story short, her check bounced, which made my check bounce and resulted in a bunch of $2 overdrafts before I realized the problem. That was terrible; a financial setback we couldn't afford. We had two girls at a time; some didn't like the situation and moved on, and then a couple of more would move in. As schooling went along, I had some scheduling that allowed me to take a job to help. One job was working for an insurance salesman, Mr. Ellis. He had another lady working for him, and at night, he would come in and rearrange all the files so we couldn't find a thing come the next day. After that job, I went to work for a Mr. Kelly, who placed part-time workers when a need arose at a business.

I went on numerous job interviews. The school said they would place you upon graduation, but in visiting with former graduates that spent long hours at the school trying to find work, I decided the best way to get a job was to read the paper and just go to businesses and ask if they had any openings. I'm not sure what took me to lawyers, but at any rate, in one—Bangs, McCullen, Buttler, and Foye—a secretary, Alice Farrington, gave me a typing test on an electric typewriter. Boy, was that a fiasco. I was used to resting my fingers heavy on the manual typewriter keys. Well, that meant you got a lot of letters you didn't expect on the electric typewriter. I didn't get that job!

One interview was at the office of Whiting, Lynn, Frieberg, and Schulz. I was being interviewed to be the secretary for Mr. Louie Frieberg. A Mr. Jackson quizzed me. He was a heavyset graying fellow with shaggy eyebrows and a gruff voice. Very intimidating to a young person. He looked me over, asked why I wanted the job, asked about my education and various questions. He then said how would they know that after I got trained for the job, I wouldn't end up pregnant. I looked him in the eye and asked, "Haven't you ever heard of contraceptives?"

I guess because I managed not to show he was scaring me to death with his attitude and actions, I was hired. I later learned that most of the lawyers didn't care much for my boss and were always looking to cause me grief just because I worked for Louie. I gained a lot of practical experience from Mr. Frieberg. He believed that I should belong to the National Secretaries Association, but at that time, I wasn't qualified to join—not enough experience. As soon as I was eligible, he paid my dues. He also had me join the Business and Professional Women's Association, always working to advance my knowledge and business savvy networking with other working women.

This was in 1965. Louie was always making connections with folks, and quite often, it would result in him taking down notes on a napkin, calling me at home, telling me where the notes were and that I needed to have two wills ready for those folks by ten the next morning. That really put pressure on me. The law firm had what was

called an MT/ST (magnetic tape/Selectric typewriter) machine that, by using two cartridges, similar to VHS tapes, a form had been typed on one cartridge and programmed to insert information from the other cartridge, made for error-free documents. One of the secretaries had input the forms on the one cartridge, and Mr. Frieberg had me learn how to run that machine so I could use it for his business, rather than using the other secretary. I put in long hours learning this on my own time but was soon able to produce wills and other documents in fine shape, error-free.

BILL CHANGES

Well, Bill sort of got the message that things weren't great on the home front, and he made some changes. No, he didn't quit drinking beer; however, he got a job as a bartender in the evenings, and when he was working, he couldn't drink, so that was wonderful. That job was short-lived. Next he got a job at a Texaco Station on Mt. Rushmore Road and Kansas City. This was when you drove into a gas station, the attendant filled your gas tank, checked the oil and water, and washed your windshield. This station also had a tow service, and Bill often was called to tow in a car to be fixed.

He had a knack for mechanical things and sometimes fell into a situation where he could purchase the car for little or nothing and make some repair and sell it for a little profit. One such car happened to have the emergency brake freeze up on some folks from New York and was broken down by Mount Rushmore. Bill called and asked me to get $50 cash to him so he could buy the car; it was a Citroen. I had to go to the bank to borrow the money since we didn't have any just laying around. The banker was very snotty and said how would we feel living out of that car. He finally gave me the money, and I took it to Bill, and we were the owners of a very used Citroen car. It was considered the French Cadillac, but the dash on this was warped from too much summer heat. It had air billows that raised it up and down, so if you needed to change a tire, you raised it up, put the jack that came with it in place, then lowered the billows, and the car was up in the air, one whole side. Our first trip in it was to the farm, then on to Gettysburg, South Dakota, to visit our friend Jim Louison and his new bride at the nursing home where they met. We were worried that the gas gauge didn't work, but when we filled it up, it got eighty-five miles to the gallon; the gauge worked perfectly.

It seemed we had a lot of cars. The first new one was a 1961 Plymouth that Bill traded his Mercury for with the help of Mom and Dad. We had Aunt Edna's Buick, a Ford Station wagon, Bill's folks' Cadillac, and a long list of many other vehicles while living in Rapid.

CLOTHES

The need for clothes for Shelley and myself was another problem. They cost money. I soon discovered some churches that had rummage sales, and quite often, I would come up with things like those full skirts with lots of material in them and a shower curtain for about 10¢ and maybe even luck out and find a batch of little elastic. From the shower curtain and elastic, I made rubber pants to go over the cloth diapers. The big skirts would make clothes for Shelley and Sandra. My sewing I learned in 4-H, and the sewing machine the folks gave us was put to good use.

I made most of my dress clothes for work and, in an evening, could whip together a skirt and blouse to wear the next day. I would do the same for the girls as they grew up. Patterns were easy for the little girls, but as they grew, I needed to buy patterns for them and myself. Eventually with lots of secondhand stores and rummage sales,

it was cheaper to purchase used clothes than it was to buy the material and a pattern. A big corduroy skirt made the jumper that matched for the girls, and a sheet made the blouses. The dress Shelley is wearing was made from the dress I graduated high school in and also wore for the picture taken at Penny's. Rarely was there any waste when I was sewing; things were even pieced together to fit a pattern.

MECHANIC SCHOOL

After Mr. Freiberg had me join the National Secretaries Association, a fundraiser that was put on was selling thirty-second radio advertisements to businesses around town. One of the businesses I was to sell ads to was Dodge Town; Milo Rypkema was the owner. Not only did Milo buy an ad from me, but he inquired how things were going. He knew my folks and had a high respect for them since Dad had bought several cars from Milo and had great fun with him. I told him it wasn't all that great. That Bill needed a better job, and didn't know what we were going to do. Well, Milo said there was a training school for mechanics that he could sponsor Bill to attend, but it was in Sioux Falls. I gathered all the information from him and took it home to Bill. He thought that was a good idea.

There were another couple of fellows from Rapid that were also signed up for the schooling, so they were able to share a ride. The one's wife and three children were living in a small rental house in Rapid.

Bill, at that time, had his folks' Cadillac car, and he drove most of the time, doing mechanic work on it. Of course, it took several cases of beer to make that long drive! They would spend the week in Sioux Falls, then drive home Friday night, then leave Sunday afternoon to go back. Usually home meant stopping at the Longbranch Bar before actually making it home.

More than once, I would stop by and, in no uncertain terms, express my anger over the fact he preferred stopping there rather than getting on home. On one trip home, in the dark of night, a pheasant flew up and hit the windshield, breaking it, and ended up in the back seat. That was one time having a beer can tipped up; drinking saved the passenger because a piece of the windshield was stopped by the can.

Bill made numerous friends at that mechanic school, but the only one that has stayed close was Dave Hunoff from Yankton. Bill was so good that he was able to work as well as go to school, so that helped out some. After the schooling was over, Milo said he didn't have a spot for Bill to work at, but he got hired on at Frontier Ford as an apprentice under another mechanic. The pay was only $1.25 an hour; not enough to live on for sure, but he was getting the experience needed. Bill quit that job because of the low pay, and he and another fellow went to work in Wyoming. He borrowed an old car from the folks. The first day on the job over there, they came around and made him procure license plates in Wyoming since he was working there. That job didn't last long because the mechanic he was working under at Frontier Ford wanted him back and offered to pay out of his own pocket $.25, making the wage $1.50. Bill returned to Ford to finish the apprenticeship and became a full-time mechanic. He did have the expense of getting a toolbox and all the necessary tools of the trade. That was an expensive proposition, but they served him well over the years, and he still has a good share of them.

While he was working that short time in Wyoming, he lost his wallet. Because he wasn't too good with handling money, I had written him a check for $10 that he could cash when he needed to. That check was in the wallet, along with his driver's license and a couple of pictures. Whoever found or took the wallet went to Spearfish and cashed the check by writing *Bill Sumpter* in the "pay to the order of" line and, using his driver's license, cashed the $10 check. The first I knew about the lost wallet was when the sheriff of Lawrence County showed up at our trailer, asking me to verify Bill's handwriting on the check; it wasn't his.

Several months later, after we had replaced the driver's license and gotten another wallet, his old boss's brother, Chet Muckler, who owned a house in Sturgis, was getting it ready to rent, and in the upstairs, there was a dresser, and Bill's wallet was in it, with all the things still in it. He got it back to us.

HOUSE HUNTING

Actually we weren't house hunting at the time, but my boss, Louie Frieberg, was a real estate agent, and there were quite a few HUD houses being sold. I was totally sick of the trailer and all the winter months thawing pipes, and he knew that, so one day, he took me out and showed me several of the houses on the market.

Most of them were in the south part of Rapid. After looking at about seven houses, I picked one on Fairmont Boulevard—130 E. Fairmont—that I liked. The price was $11,000, and if you qualified, your name would be put in a hat, and whoever's name was drawn out got first chance to buy it. That evening, we got Bill to go along and look at the same houses, and by golly, he picked the same one I did. As luck would have it, we got to buy that house under an FHA loan. This house had a crawl space and all hardwood floors in the bedrooms. There were three bedrooms, a see-through opening between the living room and kitchen, an entryway where there was the washer and dryer and furnace, a big backyard, with a big hill and no alley. The grade school was Grandview, and it was walking distance. I found a babysitter not too far from the school, so the move was great since school in the valley would have been a problem. That was in 1964.

When we made the move from Rapid Valley into town, we didn't realize the entertainment we had furnished to the truckers that worked across the street from us. They told us they used to sit out on the trucks to listen to the battles going on at our place! I can imagine they heard plenty when I was so mad at Bill.

While I was attending school at the National College of Business and subsequently got a job, I would stop and pick up Kay Muckler and take her to her beauty school in the morning. Her folks picked her up in the afternoon. That saved them a trip. Kay was done with school by the time we moved into town. Our trailer and the land was eventually sold, and the money was paid back to Mom and Dad.

Dad had made a bid to tear down the old Marietta School, which was northwest of the farm, and clean up the remnants of it. Back in the day, it was quite a school; a two-story building and a dormitory where many from the community boarded for school. There was a lot of good lumber in that old school, and most of the 2'×4's were 14 feet long. Bill and I, Dad, and Uncle Clint (Dad's brother) spent several weekends reclaiming that lumber, hauling away the bricks, and stacking them at the farm, along with other things that needed to be cleaned up. The lumber came up to Rapid, and Uncle Clint proceeded to build us

a big oversized four-car garage that was 14' tall in 1969, on Fairmont Boulevard.

As broke as we always seemed to be, we had a great selection of cars over the years. Upon trading off Bill's Mercury for a 1961 Plymouth, which we hung onto until 1964, then it seemed we floated from one car to another. Here we are in the summer of 1963, with Bill's mother, Virgie, and stepfather, Erby Melton, who came to visit us.

We had a great time showing them around the area. One thing they wanted to do was to get us all shoes as a gift, something practical. It was easy to get Bill shoes, and Shelley, but when it came to me, I was so used to being barefoot that it was really hard to find anything that would fit. Finally Erby asked the store clerk if they had a couple of shoeboxes they could put me in. Back in that day, size 10 wide shoes were not that abundant. After we moved to Fairmont Boulevard, we had a 1960 Ford van, which we used to go to Pactola and Angustora by Hot Springs.

We put many miles on that rig, even taking it as far as Arkansas. After Bill got the job at Frontier Ford, it seemed that we had quite a bit of access to used cars. We tried to figure out just when the 1961 Plymouth went away.

During some of those times, we had Aunt Edna's 1956 Oldsmobile, Bea and Butch's (Bill's dad and stepmom) 1957 Cadillac, a 1956 Buick, a 1959 Ford station wagon, which we took on our first trip to Arkansas in 1966. Then along came a 1963 Rambler American hardtop, which we think we traded the Plymouth for.

No, you are not seeing double! One day, Bill looked out the door at Frontier Ford and saw what he thought was our car. *Had I traded it off?* He asked about it, and it was a new trade-in, so he bought it and brought it home and parked it in the driveway. Since I always parked in the garage, I was upset that he had parked my car outside when he wanted me to look

out the door. What a surprise—we had twin cars. Sometimes when I would go to work, I would get teased because my car had been parked at the bar where they saw it. I then knew where Bill had spent some time that night for sure. Our neighbors called and thought they had been drinking too much since they were seeing identical cars parked in our garage. During this time, we also had motorcycles. One was a Jawa, but it was a tall motorcycle, and I had trouble keeping it up. One time, it laid over with me, and the muffler burned my leg pretty bad. I quit riding it after that. Then there was a Triumph, and it seemed that motorcycle went through pistons every time we went on a long ride.

We found a white Honda Dream that was pretty well used up for me to learn to ride on. We took it for a ride on the hills behind the School of Mines, and I missed a gear at a critical time going up the hill and laid it over to the right, on the upside of the hill. Bill was already way ahead of me, with the girls riding with him. I grabbed the bike to set it up, and it flopped over on the downhill side, with me hanging on. Another biker helped me get it set up again. After I learned to ride that junker, we found a beautiful black Honda Dream, and I rode it quite often with the girls on it. It was economical to ride, better than the car in nice weather.

Our neighbors that lived to the west and had a bedroom that was right beside our driveway were Bill and Ruth Schell and their three kids. Bill was a highway patrolman, and one night my Bill and his friend Ken Hartman had come home on the motorcycles and parked in our drive. When Ken was ready to leave for his home, he and Bill were pretty drunk and boisterous in our driveway, and Ken couldn't even get the key in the ignition. Later, Bill Schell said he was about ready to get out of bed and put the damned key in the ignition for him to get some sleep. We got along fine with that family.

We had a pet rabbit in a setup in the backyard, and one stormy night, I went out to check on the rabbit and found a very cold little boy back there. I brought him in and warmed him up and called the police about finding him; he was only about two or three and didn't talk well. The good Lord sent me out at the right time because that little fellow wouldn't have lived had I not found him. The girls wanted to keep him, since they got to keep cats and dogs that were strays. I had to explain you just don't keep kids!

On our trip to Arkansas in 1966, we brought back a little puppy—part basset hound and beagle. His coloring was beagle, and his little legs were basset. He was called Boots. Well, one winter night, Boots got away from us. In an effort to find him, I got in the car and was driving slow and calling for him, circling the block.

Somewhere along the way, Boots heard me and was running along behind the car in the snow. Bill and the girls finally saw him and got him off the street, and I got home, thinking I couldn't find him.

On our way home from Arkansas in our van, we stopped in Huron, at the state fair where Mom and Dad had their Airstream trailer parked. They had come for the entire week of activities. When we got there, it was 110. We put Boots in the air-conditioned trailer and went out to do some things at the fair with the girls. When we went back in the trailer, Boots was cooled down, and fleas were jumping all over him. That gave us a clue he needed to have a flea collar. We traveled in the cool of the evening to the farm and spent the night there. When we got up the next morning, there were seven inches of snow on the ground. What a difference from the day before at Huron and 180 miles. This was the first of September.

HOUSE GUESTS

Well, I guess we will call them house guests, but some came and stayed a long time, and others, it was a brief encounter.

Bill would pick me up from work, and we would go home, and I'd fix lunch. This one day, when I went to get in the van, there was a young man already there. We went home, and I fixed lunch for us all, and Bill announced that this was Rich Cordwel, who just started work at Frontier Ford, and he was going to live with us for a while. Well, Rich lived with us for quite a few years.

Bill's mechanical ability seemed to apply mostly to cars. The dryer quit working, so he decided to tear into it and see what was wrong. He had it strung all over the entryway and hadn't discovered the remedy to get it fixed, and because he didn't do the laundry, he wasn't in a real hurry to put things back together. The entire household put up with that mess in the entryway. Bill was still going to the bar after work, so he wasn't too worried about the dryer. Finally I got fed up with it and called Montana Dakota Utilities and inquired if they had a dryer, would they take away the old one, and how soon could they deliver. By the end of the day, about a month after the old dryer had been torn apart, we had a new dryer. If you want something done, sometimes you have to take the bull by the horns and get it done.

Another drinking buddy of Bill's had left his wife. For some reason, he ended up with a tall five-drawer dresser and another dresser with six drawers and a mirror when he left. He moved in at our place and gave us the dressers, which were full of dust. He slept on the couch for quite a while until he found a place to live, not wanting the dressers back. We still have them.

WHERE WERE YOU?

It was a cold November day, and I had reported in at work at the law firm of Whiting, Lynn, Freiberg, and Schulz, but when Mr. Freiberg came into the office, he noticed I wasn't feeling good, so he sent me home. I'm not sure if I had a cold coming on or what, but I left the girls with the babysitter and tucked myself into bed to get some much-needed rest and try to kick the cold that was penetrating the air around me. I turned the radio in the bedroom on to listen to music until I could drift off to sleep.

I was just twenty-one and was proud to have voted in the general election when I turned eighteen. Our country had just averted a nuclear disaster during the Cuban Missile Crisis under the Cold War with the Soviet Union. Our president, John F. Kennedy, had established the Peace Corps—which provides support to countries around the world—as well as the Apollo program, with the goal of beating the Soviet Union in the Space Race. This president was young and energetic and had a way to get things accomplished.

As I lay snuggled up under the covers with the radio on, instead of the usual music, it was a special broadcast telling about President Kennedy and First Lady Jackie in a motorcade in downtown Dallas, when all of a sudden, there was a news flash. At 12:30 p.m. Central Standard Time, November 22, 1963, our president was shot and killed. All a person could do was listen in shock and disbelief. That moment was frozen in my mind. I remember exactly where I was and how I was unable to turn away from the television, watching it all happen over and over as the news media kept the networks flooded with every detail of this tragic day. The assassination of this president sent shock waves around the world. He was the second youngest president of this nation, and his famous words reverberate, "Ask not what your country can do for you but what you can do for your country." Where were you?

TOGETHER

As I stated before, we did bowl together. Of course, there was beer available there for Bill. It was a rather costly evening out, what with the fee for bowling and the drinks and babysitter, but at least we were doing something together.

When we were growing up, Dad and Mom would bring us to Rapid for dance lessons, and I loved to dance. With Bill's consent, I had signed us up for lessons with the Arthur Murray dance studio. This seemed like something that might be fun, and we could do together. Well, we showed up for one lesson, and there were other fees associated with the lessons we had agreed to, and Bill dug his heels in and said he wasn't going to go anymore. Now what to do? We had signed up for the lessons, and they wanted their money. Finally I was able to negotiate with them and get the contract cancelled, saying that we couldn't pay, and that we hadn't taken any of the lessons so could they just forget about it? They finally did, but I still would have liked for Bill to learn how to ballroom dance.

WORK

Even though we both were holding down full-time jobs, it seemed we were tight for money. Maybe it was because too much went for beer and cigarettes! At any rate, I started typing dissertations for students at the School of Mines. I can't recall just how I happened to get these jobs, but it paid 10¢ a page. I did this at home in the evening, at the kitchen table. One night, a student came with some corrections, and the only place we could go over the material was in the bedroom. The living room was full of folks watching TV, and the girls were doing things in the kitchen. That particular material was in French and Mexican, and I really had to work to do the words because they were unfamiliar to me, and I had to manually add squiggles with ink where needed. He got an A on it and was plenty pleased with the work I had done.

Meanwhile, back at the law office, things weren't the best. My boss, Louie Frieberg, was attorney for Gate City Creamery, and they were going out of business. Because there was a worry that things would disappear from misappropriation by employees, Mr. Frieberg had me go in to work there early morning, way before my regular hours, and work there all day.

This arrangement went on for several weeks. Mr. Lynn was always looking for ways to cause trouble for Mr. Freiberg, and my absence from the office gave him some ammunition. As soon as I was back at the office, he called me in and said there was a red flag out, and I was to be on notice that I could be fired. That was not very comforting, to say the least. Already I had been reprimanded for not having my high heels on after running to the courthouse for Mr. Frieberg to file some papers, and when I got back in my cubicle, I had forgotten to change shoes, and Mr. Lynn walked by a door and saw that. He called me on the phone to advise me that the secretaries wore heels and nylons at *all* times.

This all happened on a Friday, when Mr. Frieberg wasn't in the office, and one of the partners called him to say Mr. Lynn had fired his secretary. Monday morning, I showed up for work, and Louie was so surprised and called me into his office immediately to find out what was going on. He was livid. How could Mr. Lynn fire his secretary! At any rate, I figured I wasn't fired and stayed on, but it was a rather hostile environment, and finally I told Louie I was going to find another job, which he didn't blame me for. Actually he was willing to quit the firm and take me with him to a new place. I told him that wouldn't be necessary for my benefit. Later, he did just that, and I helped him get his office set up along with his new secretary.

I always told my boss if he was going to fire me, give me two minutes to quit first! In that day and age, I don't think there was such a thing as workman's comp or unemployment insurance. At any rate, my last day on the job, Mr. Frieberg and his wife, Lucille, and Judge Tut Shaw and his wife wanted to take Bill and me out to the Elks Club for supper and dancing. Well, guess where Bill was after work—at the Longbranch Bar. This wasn't going to stop them from taking us out for supper, so we pulled into the Longbranch, and Louie (the lawyer) and Mr. Shaw (the judge) went in and, with one on each side of Bill, took his arms and ushered him out to the car, only saying for those in the bar to hear, "You're coming with us, Bill." Boy, did his friends think he was in a lot of trouble. We had a good evening, and Bill, in his greasy work clothes, danced with the two ladies that were dressed for the occasion.

My Bosses

Louie Freiberg was a fairly heavy man with a gruff voice. He had been a county commissioner in Pennington County and also served in the House of Representatives in South Dakota before I went to work for him. He was loud spoken and said what he thought. You have to remember, I was all of twenty-one when I went to work for him. He pushed me to learn many of the tools of the trade, and with his confidence in me, I also gained confidence. Like I said, he felt networking was essential to growth, and that was why he paid my dues to the National Secretaries Association and the Business and Professions Women's Association. I made the time to attend the meetings, be involved, and gained a lot from them.

One time, I remember I made a mistake on something I had done for Mr. Freiberg, and he jumped right in the middle of me.

I replied, "Well, I thought—"

And he interrupted me with, "I'm not paying you to *think*." After he said it and things cooled down, he apologized; he really did want me to *think*.

He and his wife adopted two boys, Kevin and Michael. They had a pretty good-sized house, and I loaned them the buggy from our Stroll-O-Chair, so Lucille or her helper could push baby Michael from room to room in comfort.

Lucille was diabetic and also had a tendency to drink. The two didn't work well, and Kevin would come home from school on occasion and find her in a coma.

Louie was generous, and at Christmas, he would gift me things clients gave to him. I always told him what he'd given me because quite often, he never even opened the boxes. I had done a lot of leather tooling when I was younger and had all the tools, so for Christmas, I made him a key case, hand-tooled and with his initials in it. The girls and I were on our way to Philip this one Christmas, and I took homemade gifts to the Frieberg house. They were having a party and insisted I and the girls come in for some treats. Louie carried that key case with him until the day he died. He also gave me some money, and I bought a La-Z-Boy recliner for Bill. When Bill came home, the girls and I were excited for him to try the chair out. He said he didn't like it; it was too this and too that. I was ready to return it to the store but then decided, heck, that was my gift; if he didn't like it, he didn't have to sit in it. He grew to like it after that.

Louie was raised a good Catholic on a ranch south of Plainview, South Dakota. He showed me a picture of a trim cowboy on a bucking horse and asked if I knew who it was. It was him in his younger days. Louie's folks gifted some of their place to the diocese of Rapid City, and they built a Native American Learning Center where three priests usually resided and held group learning conferences.

He took me there and showed me around the place several times. He told me that if he had anything to confess, he always went to a Catholic church out of the area.

This office was on the second story of the First National Bank in Rapid City. There were numerous other offices along the way to the bathrooms. We were given fifteen-minute breaks twice a day, and because I didn't drink coffee or smoke, I would visit with the secretaries in the other offices to and from the bathroom. Finally I decided I would drink coffee. It was free in the office, and you could get refills in a café, so I started drinking coffee at age twenty-one. Usually it was cold coffee because I would get engrossed in whatever I was doing and forget to take a drink.

After spreading the word around among the secretaries, I found a job with Charles (Charlie) Carroll and Al Scovel of Carroll and Scovel, whose office was in the Melgren building on Kansas City Street, second floor. I was the only secretary they had and did all of the things associated with an office—bookkeeping, cleaning, typing letters and documents, updating legal books, etc. It was quite a busy time but a fun time. Charlie and Al had a daily routine of going to coffee at the

Alex Johnson Hotel every afternoon. One afternoon, there was a guy in gorilla costume advertising for the movie at the Elks Theatre across from the coffee shop. Al said that gorilla's nose looked like Charlie's; you could put your fists in there and shake them around.

Well, Charlie wanted to get even with Al for his jokes about his nose, so he asked me to see if we could hire the fellow in costume to come and play a joke on Al. I went on a mission and soon had things all lined up for the joke. I buzzed Al that he was supposed to get into Charlie's office immediately; he was really mad about something. In the meantime, the man in the gorilla costume was seated in Charlie's chair, and the door to the office was closed, and Charlie was in the library that joined his office. Al came out of his office and was giving me instructions about something or other to look busy and was sort of backing into Charlie's office as he spoke, not looking really where he was going. Boy, was he ever surprised when he turned around, and the gorilla was there.

We all had a good laugh over that. The man in the costume never got out of character, just played his part. We had a petty cashbox, and it seemed they were always getting money out of it, and I was supposed to keep track of where it went. Finally I taped a rubber band onto some of the bills so when they took the money out, it sprung back into the box.

Here I am with flowers the guys gave me during secretaries' week. I wore wigs then and had a couple of colors.

It wasn't too long before I was looking for another job. Mr. Carroll was asked to be a judge, and he couldn't refuse such a good job, so he and Al dissolved their partnership, and Al went to a bigger firm.

In the same building, there was a psychiatrist, Harold Henrie, and he needed a secretary, so I just moved a few doors down in the same building and went to work for him. He was the only psychiatrist in the entire area so was very busy. In fact, he hired a part-time gal to work from five in the evening until nine. He came from Maryland with his family. He had a family of six children and a big dog. Dr. Henrie said that psychiatrists have about as many problems as their patients, and that was really true of him. I tried to keep him out of trouble as best I could, and he had a lot of confidence in me. At one time, he gave me a gun to keep in my desk drawer. He said if I heard shots in his office, to shoot whoever came out.

He laced his coffee with whiskey, and most generally, on a certain day of the week, I might as well figure he wasn't going to work the rest of the afternoon because he was going to drink with a patient that should not be drinking.

One winter day, he sent me to the local clothing store, Blumenthals, with money in hand to buy his patient—a married woman he was having an affair with—a pair of sunglasses. It was a warm day in late February, and to go the few blocks in Rapid City, I didn't even need a coat. When I got to the store and purchased the glasses, I noticed they were having a great sale on winter coats. One coat caught my eye; it had a real sheep wool collar and wool around the bottom of the sleeves. It was a nice brown Naugahyde, fake leather, and fit like a glove. I didn't have any identification or money and asked if I could put it aside and come back later to pay for it. The saleslady was so trusting and handed me the coat to take for approval, not knowing who I was, where I lived, or anything.

Now I had a spiffy new coat to wear on approval. As I headed for home, I saw that Bill was at the local bar, so I pulled in and walked into the bar wearing this new coat. Now Bill rarely said anything about clothes, or I wondered if he ever even noticed, but he did take note of this new coat. He asked me where I got it, and when I told him I had it on approval from the store, he said, "I don't approve!" What? This man never said something like that to me. Well, here he was, surrounded by all his friends, so I pulled out a chair, stepped up on it, then to the tabletop, let out a sheep-herding whistle to get everyone's attention, then modeled the coat from the table and asked if anyone approved of it. The vote was unanimous approval.

As I stepped back down to the floor, I looked at Bill and said, "I don't need your approval. It's mine." The next day, I went to the store and paid for it.

It was as if I was in a soap opera when I took the job with Dr. Henrie. There was a lot of drama from day to day. Not only because of the patients he saw but because of the things he did. Because he was the only psychiatrist in town, on a regular basis, deputies would escort prisoners into the office for an evaluation as to their sanity, whether they were competent to stand trial and such.

Dr. Henrie was hard to get to dictate the information for each file, and I had to constantly keep after him about that. I even learned to crotchet on his time, thinking that would prompt him to get the work to me; it somewhat worked. I only got one scarf made by following instructions in a *Teach Yourself to Crotchet* book. He was quick to prescribe pills or hand out samples salesmen gave him. We had one lady from the air base that he was seeing, and she was terrified about turning thirty. She was a regular patient, had two young children and a military husband. She made sure she didn't have to worry about being thirty; she overdosed on pills she had been saving.

Dr. Henrie was abusive to his wife and cheated on her. One time, because I knew he was going to be with one of the patients, I called his wife and suggested she get a babysitter, and Bill and I would take her out for supper. We saw Mr. Frieberg when we were at supper and invited him along as we went to a few bars. When we took her home, Dr. Henrie was there; she had us all come in, and we stayed into the wee hours of the morning, afraid to leave her alone with him. Finally we had to go home. I was at work early; his wife called and, in a hushed voice, told me he was coming in and to be prepared for anything. He had punched holes in the wall and, I'm sure, hit her. One of the older children had told him we were going out. Finally in desperation to get away from him, she loaded up all the kids and dog in their station wagon and left the country. She had family in Canada mail things back to get a divorce, not letting him know where she was. I think it saved her life. He was mad at me, too, but knew better than to try anything.

During this divorce, Dr. Henrie made threats to the lawyer handling her divorce as well as the judge. It wasn't too long after that Dr. Henrie was arrested and sent to Yankton, South Dakota, where those with mental illness are housed for an evaluation. He was detained for several weeks. At one point, he was free to go and was at the airport, waiting for a flight back to Rapid City, when he was taken back into the facility for further evaluation. After that happened, he called me to bring the checkbook, ask Bill to come along and drive his car there. This time, he kept the car and paid for our plane trip back to Rapid. If he got released again, he was going to be long gone in the car before someone changed their mind.

He was a poor money manager, and because I did the check-writing, he told me to always be sure I got paid first. Finally the day came when there was no money in the bank, and he wasn't working, so I told him he had to close his office. He went to another state and opened up an office for a while and, in the end, committed suicide. My final pay was a filing cabinet and some office things.

Here I was, looking for another job at the ripe old age of twenty-nine. All of the above bosses still liked me and would have given me a job in a minute, but they had gone on and gotten other secretaries. Again my connections with the secretaries helped me out, and I had an interview with Attorney Ramon Roubideaux. He wanted to interview me in a very public place, so we met at a café in good daylight. He was French Indian and was a recovering alcoholic, he informed me.

He hired me on the spot. I was supposed to work with the secretary that was leaving until she had shown me what needed to be done. That training lasted all of half a day; I knew more than she could teach me. Ramon had also been a secretary, so he knew a lot about the day-to-day things. However, the first day I was by myself, he dictated a lot of letters to get sent that day. I would just set up the paper and type as I listened to the Dictaphone. Usually if you take the time to listen to the content of the letter, you space it lower or higher on the paper. When he signed off on each letter, he commented that it should be lower, the spacing would be better different, etc. As I was closing up the office that night, his old secretary from a few years before called, wondering if he was looking for a secretary. I told her to call him at home because he had left for the day. I also told her this was my first day on the job, and if he wanted her, that would be fine. I no sooner got home that Ramon called to tell me he wanted me to keep working for him.

This is me at my desk in Ramon's office

It was during my time working for Ramon that the Pine Ridge Indians took over occupancy at Wounded Knee, February 27, 1973, also known as the Second Wounded Knee. Two main ones involved in that were Dennis Banks and Russell Means. The American Indian Movement (AIM) originated in 1968, arising from the concerns of Native Americans in Minneapolis, Minnesota. AIM focused on changing the life of Indians in the urban environment. Clyde Bellecourt and Dennis Banks, Chippewa from Minnesota, assisted in the creation of AIM. Later, Russell Means, an Oglala Sioux, became one of the more aggressive leaders of the organization.

AIM leaders and about two hundred supporters, en route to Porcupine, South Dakota, stopped at the village of Wounded Knee and took over the trading post, museum, gas station, and several churches. Those involved in the takeover considered Wounded Knee historically significant and deemed the village an appropriate location from which to voice the concerns of AIM and the Oglala Sioux of the Pine Ridge Reservation. The takeover, on February 27, 1973, marked the beginning of a conflict between AIM and the US government that lasted until May 8, 1973. The occupation of that little village went on for seventy-one days. Senators Jim Abourezk and George McGovern, along with two aides for President Kennedy, were on hand the day after this occupation to negotiate release of hostages and come to an agreement.

During the occupation of Wounded Knee, the natives laid waste to the buildings and property. They had several attorneys assisting them from Minnesota and eventually came to the office of my boss, Ramon Roubideaux, and got him involved in the matter.

Mr. Roubideaux was proud of the fact that he had been sober for over fifteen years. He was also cautious about panhandling Native Americans coming to his office to get a handout. When I first started working for him, he gave me a list of his family members. He advised me that if others came by saying they were cousins or such, to send them on their way.

His mother, Eva Nichols, had an office in the same building and was a great advocate for helping her people in a very positive way, with job placement and resources to help themselves.

After Ramon accepted helping Dennis Banks and Russell Means, our office was busy with folks coming and going. I heard the two above tell him there was no reason he couldn't have a drink. "Was it the white man that told you, you couldn't drink?" Finally Ramon gave in, and as you know, one drink is too much, and there is never enough.

When Banks and Means were coming into the office, they treated me badly, and I finally told Mr. Roubideaux that I was not going to stand for being treated like white trash; I was going to have to quit. He promptly put a stop to them even coming by my desk, using a back door to his office.

Our mailbox was at the post office, and folks from the East Coast began sending boxes upon boxes of clothing. I had to open them and check to be sure there were no firearms or explosives, then they were

sent with folks to Wounded Knee. The compassion the folks showed by sending good clothes to help only ended up thrown in piles and slept on or destroyed.

I was busy typing agreements and all sorts of pleadings during this occupation. Ramon was thrown into continual drinking, and as he became less effective, they soon pushed him aside, leaving a crushed individual in their wake.

While folks waited to get in to see Ramon, Banks, or Means, I would visit with them. Several of the people confided to me that after they had occupied Wounded Knee, for a certain length of time, they got to go R & R in the Soviet Union. I told them that while they were there to check out how many people of different cultures were seen. They never reported back to me on that.

Ramon never recovered completely from this encounter. I was soon, more or less, handling things in the office and negotiating open files with other attorneys. I enjoyed that aspect of my job and started to study to become a paralegal.

Each of my jobs were learning experiences that no school could ever prepare you for.

OUTDOORS

The girls spent a great amount of time outdoors. The television was not something that occupied the daylight hours. Summer and winter there was always something to do. Shelley loved to play in the snow, and Sandra got to enjoy it as well. They had their constant dog company of Lady when we lived in the valley. It was a time of carefree playing without worry because the neighbors were always on the watch for the little ones, as well as us parents. We were still young inexperienced people, learning on a daily basis about how to be good parents and raise healthy happy girls.

We had a washing machine in the trailer but no dryer, so I had to hang clothes out, summer or winter or whatever the weather was, except rain of course. In the winter, it took some preparation and several trips to the clothesline to get everything hung up. First, I would shake out each cloth diaper and lay them together and, after putting on my coat, would put the batch over one arm, so when I made a dash for the clothesline in the freezing weather, I could grab an end, stick a clothespin in it, pull it to the next end, another clothespin, etc., until the last of the diapers were hung up. Next trip in to warm up, I did the same with the tails of shirts, pants were hung by the waistband, socks and underwear next. By then, usually the diapers were freeze-dried and could come back in.

Bedsheets were a real challenge because you needed to have them folded in the middle and gathered on your arm to get enough clothespins to keep them on the line in the wind, which always seemed to blow. Of course, the lines had to be wiped down before you hung anything out because birds had a tendency to sit on the wires. I was thankful for the washing machine; it made life so much easier and really beat hauling clothes in the back seat of the car, waiting to find enough money to use a Laundromat. In the summer, the girls were outside helping me in the garden or just playing with the neighbor kids. When we moved to Fairmont Boulevard, they soon found kids in the neighborhood to play with, ride bikes, and walk to the store, which was down the street from our place.

At our place on Fairmont Boulevard, there was always something going on; either the girls and I were doing yard work, housecleaning, or visiting the neighbors. Shelley was in Brownies and needed a uniform. To scrounge up the money for that was a real problem, and I discovered that at a department store in town, they sold used ones that were donated to them. I did finally get her outfitted, and she attended those meetings, and I helped the leader as best I could. We had constant visits from two little neighbor girls, and they never seemed in a hurry to go home; I always had to send them home so we could have supper. I finally went and met their mother. The house was a mess inside, and they had cockroaches scurrying around the kitchen in plain sight. It was no wonder those girls wanted to be at our place. I was working as a legal secretary, and Bill was full-time at Frontier Ford.

We rode motorcycles with friends, and the girls would be with us. They were so comfortable on the motorcycle that you would feel the helmet slide out of the middle of your back; a nudge would wake the sleeper up enough to hold on tighter. Usually these were longer trips when they would sleep.

Shelley and her friends rode bicycles a lot, and once, she decided to go flying down a steep hill and lost control, came home banged up pretty bad, but that didn't stop her from riding again as soon as she got bandaged up.

The big hill behind the house on Fairmont was fair game for lots of winter fun. The girls had a saucer sled and would pull it to the top of the hill and come flying down. The first few times, they didn't know to steer with their feet and crashed into the cement step. That was not a good deal. I gave them motherly suggestions on stopping, and off they went to try again. The real worry was that they would fly out into the busy street because that hill gave them a lot of power. They always managed to get stopped before the street and to avoid the step. After we built the garage, the great run on the sled was interrupted.

GARBAGE DISPOSAL

Mom and Dad had purchased a place in a fourplex in Sun City, Arizona, and it had a garbage disposal. When you live in the country and have chickens, you don't need such a thing, but living in town makes it handy to dispose of things as you clean out the refrigerator. After her experience with the garbage disposal, Mom thought that would be something I would like.

Because our house seemed very small for our family of four and our new boarder Rich, we looked around for a bigger house we might be able to afford. The little house on Fairmont was about 940 square feet, but then there was the wonderful garage we had built. It wasn't attached, but it was great to be able to keep things in out of the weather and safe and secure.

Our house hunting took us to North Rapid, the corner of Anamosa and Greenbriar Streets. There was an elementary school just five or six blocks from home, a middle school within walking distance, and a Baptist Church right across the street. The house had a full basement, unfinished with three bedrooms on the upper level, and was on a corner lot. It was for sale through the FHA for $17,000. The Realtor said because our other house was FHA, he didn't think we would succeed in getting this one, but we put in a bid at any rate. Guess what? We got the loan and the house. Now what to do? We had two house payments.

We weren't satisfied to not have a garage, so the first thing I did was get a building permit to build a garage, and we got a contractor to put up the garage and do cement work for the driveway and garage floor. When I went for the building permit, they wanted us to build it, so we would have to back out onto Anamosa Street—a very busy street. I had to argue with them about placing it so we could back out onto Greenbriar Street. We decided to rent the house on Fairmont

Boulevard, only asking what the house payment was. We were scared we may not be able to make ends meet with this new purchase.

The good news was when Mom and Dad called, I told her, "Hey, guess what? We got a garbage disposal! It only cost us $17,000." Then I went on to explain about buying a new house that had a garbage disposal. The first thing I learned was not to put a whole lot of peels down it. I put potato peels in it and probably didn't run enough water. At any rate, it caused a backup of gunk in the basement.

It's amazing how the mind doesn't keep a lot of things. I don't recall exactly the year we made that move, maybe 1969 or 1970. I don't even remember all the work associated with moving. All I know is that the girls had each picked colors they wanted for their rooms, and I painted their walls and lucked out and found material to make curtains that had the same colors in them.

I do remember that the move was fast because we wanted to rent or sell the other house so we didn't get into a lot of financial difficulty. The fellow that worked at Ford, Rich, made the move with us. I think we were adopted. We also were adopted by a black-and-white cat, full grown when he came to our door on Fairmont Boulevard. The girls loved that big old cat, and he, in turn, loved them. He tolerated Bill and hated all men. He never had a litter box, just asked to go out and then would meow by our bedroom window when he wanted in. The girls named him Conoco, the hottest cat going.

On occasion, Bill and Conoco would be arriving home about the same time late at night. As the cat would walk by Bill, he would say, "So where have you been until this time of night?" The cat seemed to understand and haughtily strolled by him, like it was none of his business. Conoco made the move to Greenbriar and settled in, instinctively knowing where our bedroom window was.

One day, he didn't come home. The girls and I went house to house looking for him. Finally one woman said she had called the animal shelter because he had been hit by a car and was on our front porch, injured. Dogs had been chasing him, and he ran into the street. I was put out that nobody tried to contact us and tell us about the incident. The animal shelter people had put him down. We were devastated.

Right away, we had to work in the basement, making a bedroom and bathroom for Rich. He got moved in with very little privacy to begin with, but it didn't take long before walls sectioned off his bedroom, and a bathroom was fixed with a shower. We eventually made another bedroom in another corner of the basement and had a large family room in the rest of it.

This house was super spacious compared to the other homes we had. On the main floor were three bedrooms, the bathroom, kitchen/dining room, and living room. For some odd reason, the other owner had installed a green corrugated fiberglass sheet between the living room and kitchen where normally, there would be a doorway. Aligned with that was a counter, then the dining room table. So if you wanted to go to the kitchen from the bedrooms, bathroom, or basement, you had to walk past this green corrugated fiberglass panel, past the counter, and navigate around the kitchen table and chairs to get to the kitchen. After a short time of dealing with this cumbersome situation, I got the crowbar and hammer and went to work. Soon we had a doorway into the kitchen. The house was efficient as far as heating went because it had baseboard radiant heat produced by a boiler. For cooling, we had a window-mounted air conditioner in the living room. There was an industrial-grade carpet in the bedrooms, hallway, and bathroom and an orange-and-yellow shag carpet in the living room that you needed to rake to make it look decent after vacuuming it. The kitchen also had carpet.

A chain-link fence went in to keep our little Boots dog safe and sound, or so we thought. The girls had friends over a lot, and the dog liked to follow them when they visited at the Metties, which was across the interstate. One day, he dug out under the fence and was struck by a car. Another loss of a family pet. After that, it seemed we collected dogs of all kinds and shapes.

We inherited a poodle from the folks I worked for; he was old and partly blind. We also had a German shepherd, border collie cross, and a Pekingese.

One day, a boy was walking a Saint Bernard dog along our street. The girls wanted to go and pet him, so I said, "Sure, but be careful." The next thing I knew, they arrived home with the dog in tow, saying the boy gave him to them. That dog was friendly, but the poodle was tormenting him and barking and nipping at him, and before we could separate them, the Saint Bernard attacked the poodle. It injured him quite bad, and he died soon after that. I put an ad in the newspaper about a found Saint Bernard, but nobody answered the ad. After about a month of feeding him, some people showed up at the door when only the girls were home and claimed the dog. It seemed to me that they would turn the dog loose, and folks would take him in and feed him, then they would find where he was and take him back, not having the expense of food for that length of time.

Having animals has responsibilities as well, and the girls had to rake and clean up the backyard of the dog poop. It was not their most enjoyable task.

FINANCES

Maybe better stated—lack of finances. From the day we were married, money had been tight and needs ongoing. We thought our daughters, Shelley and Sandra, would have to get jobs to pay off their being born because we didn't have anything like insurance.

As I said before, I tried to keep a close eye on groceries to be sure the money covered the items we needed.

In high school, Ms. Noack, later Mrs. Chuck Kroetch, tried to instill the fine art of bookkeeping into her students, and it was all Greek to me. I didn't understand debit and credit as put forth in the classroom or, for that matter, any of the mathematics. After we got married, I attended the school of hard knocks and had to learn how to juggle the money to meet the bills.

There was a small grocery store that would allow you to charge groceries. It was Hermanson's in Rapid City, and we also had a service station that allowed us to charge gas; however, those bills had to be paid monthly. The good news was we didn't starve between paychecks or have to walk. The bad news was it was hard to come up with the money to pay off these charges so we could use the credit again when the money ran out before the month.

We joined the Elks Club when we got some Christmas money one year, paid the dues, which expired in about a month after we joined. We got at least one or two times to use it before we had to wait for more Christmas money the next year. Why did we even think we wanted to belong to the Elks? They did have good reasonable food and live dance music. I guess that was it.

In an effort to figure out debit and credit, I fixed up a 3×5 index card with first of the month and middle-of-the-month expenses. I put down our income, then figured out what bills needed to be paid the first of

the month; that went on one side. The rest were on the other side. It reminded me for sure what was needed.

Bill had a tendency to write checks at Buzzes Bottle Shop and not tell me about it. One time, for sure his check beat my grocery check to the bank, and it was an overdraft. Not just an overdraft where they paid the check but a charge for the overdraft, and they sent the check back to the grocery store, who called me to tell me to come with cash and pick it up. Needless to say, I was furious when I found out it was the check to the bottle shop that caused this problem. After I got it straightened out, I went to the bottle shop and proceeded to tell the clerk, in no uncertain terms, that Bill was not on the checking account anymore, and any checks they accepted from him were *no good*.

Do you think that detoured them from taking checks from him? Not at all, and when I refused to make them good, they turned them over to a collection agency. Again, I was forced to figure out what didn't get paid so I could pay off these bad checks.

Bill was a little disgusted that he never had a pocket full of money to stop at the bar with. Sometimes he didn't even have a quarter to get in a pool game and win a beer. He was a good pool shooter, and usually, he could get his drinks that way. At any rate, he said he wanted money. I handed him all the bills, my index card, and the checkbook and turned him loose at the table, telling him any money leftover he could have. After he struggled for about an hour trying to figure out a way to put some money in his pocket, he handed the mess back to me and never asked again, just got better at playing pool.

A lesson learned: never keep your register while paying bills and get distracted. One time, I was being so careful keeping a running account in the register with each check I wrote, but I got distracted, and when I was paying the minimum amount due to JCPenney, I made the fatal error of using the figure that was the entire amount of money in our account. Needless to say, that check, when cashed, overdrew our account. I went straight to the bank and went over the checks with them, thinking in the back of my mind that Bill had written another check. When I discovered I had made that terrible mistake, I went directly to Penney's to ask for a refund. They were a bit difficult to convince I needed back all but the payment that was due. Finally after taking my plea all the way to the head manager, they refunded the difference, and I put it in the bank, and whew, the bank was lenient, so the overdraft charges were cut in half.

BILL

We decided early on in this relationship that opposites attract, and much adjusting was needed to get along. However, Bill was quiet, a true Southern boy. When we got married, I told him to cut out that Southern drawl; he was in the North now. All the girls liked to listen to him talk. He did quite quickly gain the northern accent.

As much as I grumbled about the drinking and smoking, that was more because it cost money, which we didn't have or needed for other things. Pictured here is Bill sporting a suit that was given to him by Lil Gocken; she cleaned for folks and would gift Bill clothes on occasion. As you can see, he has his faithful beer and cigarette, but look at that smile. I said Lil only gave him clothes so he would undress for her.

One time, I was really frustrated with Bill and was about to throw in the towel. He stayed out late and didn't bother to let me know, and it wasn't changing. Meals would grow cold waiting for him. There was little fun in being married if I was only going to be the responsible one.

My boss said, "Well what does he do?"

I said he *doesn't* take out the trash, he *doesn't* clean the house, he *doesn't* get the groceries, he *doesn't* mow the lawn, he *doesn't* wash the car, he *doesn't* help take care of the girls, and the list seemed endless. Well, what good can you find? I thought about some of our other married friends and what their lives were like. Well, Bill never raised a hand against me, ever. He never objected to anything I did; in fact, he

would say, "You can do anything you want as long as you don't make me do it." With those two positive things in mind, I stuck it out.

Life is 10 percent what you make it and 90 percent how you take it. It was time for me to make use of the 90 percent. I soon discovered that he was *not* housebroken! By that, I mean he failed to put the seat down on the toilet. (I was more than thankful that he raised the seat so it wasn't wet on.) More than once, I would need to use the bathroom after he had gotten home late and would find myself on the cold porcelain ring with my butt in the water. I am so happy to say he is and has been officially housebroken for many years. One night, late after he got home, little Shelley, about two, had gotten up to use the bathroom, and when I went in to see if she needed help, I found her clinging to the porcelain ring, trying not to fall into the toilet. I went back in the bedroom and dragged Bill out of bed to see what leaving the seat up was like for his little daughter. After that, he never has left the seat up.

Mom and Dad had given us an old swivel rocker to help with furniture. One evening, when Bill was watching TV, the chair just broke; it leaned to one side. All he did was get up off it and moved to the couch, never even trying to fix it. The next day, I turned it over and found that a bolt in the bottom had broken, got another bolt, and fixed it. One thing I thank Bill for is because of him, I learned to be very self-sufficient in fixing things.

The sad part of all the times he spent at the bar was he missed a lot of the girls growing up. I think I also missed a lot of their growing up because I was doing the work for us both and didn't have time to sit back and just enjoy being with them. There was always something that needed to be done. I tried to be a good mother but probably failed miserably because of that.

EMPTY NEST

It was in 1966 that Mom and Dad found themselves with a total empty nest.

Kent and his wife, Nina, and daughter Arlene had come back to the ranch to see about working with Dad. Their second daughter, Debra, was born in Philip shortly after they had returned. The country life was not for Nina. The folks, in order to give the young couple space, had moved into the house in Philip, and Dad even took a job with the Production Credit Association as a fieldman. He would stop out at the ranch and offer his expertise and see how things were coming. It didn't take Kent and family long to decide he was going to re-enlist in the navy. They moved on and made that a career.

Bruce was married August 4, 1962, and he and his new bride moved to the ranch. Mom and Dad decided living in town was not the best situation, so they bought a trailer house and established a home for Bruce and Lois. Bruce bought some cattle as time went along. They were blessed with baby Janelle, then Todd. They enjoyed friendship with many of Bruce's classmates and got together with them frequently. Even with that network of friends, there was friction on the home front and sort of out of the blue, Bruce consigned his entire herd of cattle, and they packed up their possessions and headed to Seattle. He landed a job immediately with Boeing. Being from the Midwest, they liked his work ethics and knowledge. Out of sixty thousand employees, Bruce stood out as a leader. Uncle Jasper, Dad's brother, wrote this letter to the folks, December 28, 1966.

Dear Wayne and Ruth,

We were pleased to get your two Xmas cards and some news. Also received checks. You should have kept the check *this year due to your heavy loss last spring… Now about Bruce: Bruce is a fine young man. I like him a lot. He has got pride and a willingness to work and gets along well with people. He has taken me as kind of a father in want of information. I have done all I could in getting him to take the right path. It took some doing to get him to take the company offer to go to school. The Co. is sending him to school for some five months with a take-home pay of approximately $100 a week. The Co. thinks a lot of him, or they wouldn't do this. Bruce bought a home, a nice home, on time, but they did not get hurt.*

As for the farm, I just don't know at this time… In a large Co. of some 60,000 employees, they need leadership, and Bruce shows that quality. There is nothing I would like to see more than to have a Fairchild stay on the ranch. I think Bruce is making a mistake in the long pull, but our children have their own lives to live, and we should not interfere too much. That's the way we feel about our children…Jasper and Betty

Bill and I were settled in Rapid City and doing quite well. He was a master mechanic at Frontier Ford, and I was a legal secretary. At times, Shelley and Sandra would spend time with Mom and Dad when we were short a babysitter, or so they could enjoy them; it was close. Also if they needed some help on the farm, Bill and I would go down on the weekend and run tractors or help however needed.

At this time, Dad decided to become a farmer. He bought two new John Deere tractors, disks, and started plowing the place up. He hired some retired ranchers/farmers to run the tractors and also had high school kids work for him after school. Times were changing. He figured that with all the sheep and cattle manure for fertilizer, it was a great opportunity to be able to get away in the winter months.

Mom and Dad had been married twenty-seven years when all this unrest took place. They were struggling in their marriage as well as with all the farm upheaval.

Mom, being an avid reader, suggested that they take some trips to explore different countries and cultures as far as agriculture was concerned. They were already involved with the South Dakota Famers Union, and some trips were booked through that organization. They joined People to People trips, and through various farm organizations, they traveled to England, Mexico, Peru, Soviet Union, China, Japan, Germany, Sweden, Denmark, and France, to mention a few. They always made friends on these trips and kept in close contact with them.

Mom on a camel ride, and Dad as well. Quite the adventurers.

Dad driving a team made up of a horse and a camel.

Dad's brother Jasper and Betty, were on an extended vacation in Morocco and invited Mom and Dad to join them. It was a great adventure. Right off the bat, there were plane delays, which got them in a day later. Uncle Jasper had been there to meet the plane two days in a row, and when he heard there was a gringo raising a fuss, he knew it must be Dad. They had a great time. There were baboons that ran wild in the streets, and Dad and Jasper were teasing them a little, which made the baboons mad; one grabbed Jasper's cap off his head and threw it down a steep ravine. They didn't tease anymore.

Ten commandments for travelers:

1. Thou shalt not expect to find things as thou hast them at home, for thou hast left thy home to find things different.

2. Thou shalt not take anything too seriously, for a carefree mind is the beginning of a fine vacation.

3. Thou shalt not let the other tourist get on thy nerves, for thou art paying out good money to have a good time.

4. Remember thy passport so thou knowest where it is at all times, for a man without a passport is a man without a country.

5. Remember to take only half the clothes you think you need and twice the amount of money.

6. Remember, if we were expected to stay in one place, we would have been created with roots.

7. Thou shalt not worry. He that worrieth hath no pleasure. Few things are ever fatal.

8. Thou shalt not judge the people of a country by the one person with whom thou hast had trouble.

9. Thou shalt not make thyself too obviously American. When in Rome, do somewhat as the Romans do.

10. Remember, thou art a guest in every land. And he that treateth his host with respect shall be treated with respect.

They also had an Airstream trailer and traveled to many Wally Byam Caravan events. They persuaded Emma and Pat to buy an Airstream, which they enjoyed for many years, traveling around the United States and Mexico.

When they returned from their trips, they would set up programs with slides, invite the general public, and tell folks about what they learned in the way of how agriculture was handled in the various countries.

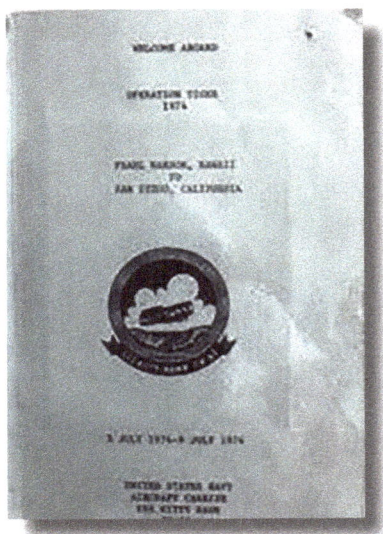

Dad was invited by Kent to ride with him on the USS Kittyhawk. What an adventure that was in 1974. Mom, Shelley, and Sandra were left at the farm to do chores.

The folks engaged in counseling to get a better perspective on their marriage, and it survived. During this time, with the coaxing from Mom, they set up a family trust and moved things into it, including the land. While I was working at the Carroll and Scovel law firm, they set up a subchapter S Corporation, established shares, and proceeded to work under this corporation umbrella. In 1972, Dad was sixty-one, and Mom was fifty-four. They were working hard but also playing hard.

There were still chickens and some cattle on the place, and neighbors were kind enough to take care of them when the folks were gone.

When it was time to haul wheat to town, Dad would load the truck, and Mom would drive it to Philip. Dad would load a second truck and meet her on the road, and they would swap trucks—him going back to the farm to load that one and Mom continuing on to the elevator. They needed help. They had one hired man for a few years, but he moved on.

THE BOOK

Who would think that a simple thing like writing down your memories and having it published would be something that would cause family division, but that is exactly what happened with Grandma Grace's family. Aunt Emma (Patterson), oldest daughter, was a stickler for detail and accuracy. She put together family genealogy that took many years and lots of travel to put together. She and Uncle Pat travelled the United States, and even England, tracking down family history and compiling it into booklets.

She wanted to know more about her mother and her memories. She felt bad because she hadn't learned firsthand from her father, Shy, about his life and his story. Emma set about getting Grace to write out her memories; this went on for several years, when Grace would spend the winters in Illinois with her. Grandma also spent time with Aunt Mildred in Wisconsin, and Aunt Mildred was aware of all the notes and writings done and asked Emma if she could have the manuscript. Mildred and Grace reviewed the things written, and finally, to get it into print and progressing, Mildred handed the manuscript over to University of Wisconsin and writer Walker D. Wyman.

Walker D. Wyman wrote this letter to Aunt Mildred, April 5, 1972:

Dear Mrs. Vesaas:

At long last the story of your mother's life in South Dakota is in print, and it has been a long struggle. The manuscript or the preface and table of contents has been sent to publishers with whom I have worked for years and in each case they have said that it is a high risk manuscript and lacks the appeal that a good piece of literature must have, if the publisher is to make back his costs of printing, etc. I have sent such materials to two other publishers for whom I have never worked, and have had the same report. This information has been sent on to you at intervals. The outlook became rather discouraging, and since this was my first such experience, I have felt it very much.

There seemed to be one thing to do: Drop the whole matter. However, I thought that the reminiscences had been retold in such a way to make them a fairly good piece of frontier literature, and decided not to accept that verdict. Therefore, I went to our local university press committee with the proposition that we publish 1,000 copies; that I would underwrite the printing cost; that if we did not sell enough to pay back the printing costs I would pay it; that the university press could take the copyright, own the book, take all or any income from it. This was agreed upon, and it is now off press. We have printed 500 paperback and 500 clothbound, but only the paperback copies have arrived. The clothback binding is done by a specialized binding firm, not the printer, and the cost is $1.20 for each book bound. They will be along in a few weeks. In the meantime, we have sent out book review copies and the various news stories will be going out this week.

Your pictures will be returned to you when they come back from the printers.

I sent two S. Dakota volumes of yours a week or two ago.

I think we (the press here) can sell enough copies to get me off of the hook, and so for the time I will keep my fingers crossed and may prayers said.

A paperback copy is being sent to you today and a clothbound will be sent when they come from the binders. The little book (shortened for this final publication) will be called a course material on the settlement of South Dakota some of these years, and unless I miss my guess, it will be

*listed by all the writers on South Dakota history as a book
telling how it was done west of the Missouri.*

Sincerely,
Walker D. Wyman

Grace writing her memories

Not only did the production of this
little 114-page book cause a division
between Emma and Mildred but also Shy's
grandson, Monty, who wrote a long letter
to the Fairchild family, objecting to the
portraying of his Grandpa Shy and father
Fred in a negative light. Fred was Shy's son
by a first marriage, so in essence, Monty
was Grace's step-grandson.

In his letter, dated August 15, 1972, he
stated:

*After reading the book which I'm sure are all discussing,
I was mad enough to challenge someone to a fist-fight,
because of the false and belittling remarks made about my
grandfather, and snide remarks about my father, so am
writing this letter to set the record straight… It seems to
me that anyone reading the book, not knowing the family,
would get the impression that mother Grace was a second
Calamity Jane or tugboat Annie type. They would gather*

that she started griping and belly-aching even before they got west of the river, and this kept on, more or less, for the next forty or fifty years. I'm sure glad that no one wrote a book of this nature about my mother... Any reader should be able to figure out that a brilliant person like Grace was made out to be would not spend forty or fifty years in that God-forsaken country with a stupid idiot like my grandfather was made out to be... Now a few words about my grandfather as I remember him. He gave me my first haircut when I was about eight years old. My mother was so mad at him for doing it she didn't speak to him for nearly a year. He was a great checker player, in fact I don't remember that any of the boys could beat him. Up to the age of about seventy-five, none of them could beat him in a foot race. The same for shooting pool. He was also an expert horse trader and I never heard of anyone getting the best of him in that department... If he hadn't had the guts for that kind of life, he wouldn't have lasted that first winter, like so many of the others that came and went. However, the one big thing he did do was the secret weapon he developed. By importing some big, fine, beautiful stallions and cross-breeding them with these little Indian ponies, he was able to supply the horse power for the ranch which meant just about everything. Without it you were dead in the water... and now for my father: When we were boys, both of our fathers were sort of joke material at times, but in the past few years I have come to appreciate how great they really were. My father was a pioneer and a good one. If he hadn't been he wouldn't have lasted thirty or forty years. Since there were no successes but only failures in those early years, due to drought and grasshoppers, or what have you, he was no bigger failure or success than anyone else... Of course my father was interested in bigger things than just plain ranching. During the twenties he got interested in organizing the farmers and ranchers into a big union so they could get a better price for the things they produced. Would you believe it, to this day those stupid farmers from coast to coast still work all year and spend money like crazy on costs like seed, fertilizer, labor, machinery, in fact everything they buy, then sit back and take whatever they are offered instead of demanding and getting their costs plus a small profit. This was one of my dads failures... He worked hard on an early woman's lib. deal called Equal rights for Women starting in 1923. Well, it finally passed in 1971. He also worked on woman's suffrage, and worked hard for workman's compensation and unemployment insurance...my Dad was making speeches around the state fighting for social security... Some people really thought he was crazy then. If any of you still think so, you might consider sending your social security checks back to Uncle Sam. Of all the ranchers in that area at that time, my Dad no doubt did more for other people than anyone else.

Aunt Emma asked if I knew where any of the books were for sale. When I said yes, she said buy them and burn them. She and Aunt Mildred were never close after the book was published. It was popular and had twelve printings in all.

HEALTH

When you are young, you don't seem to be too concerned with your health. It just isn't something that knocks on the door and says, *Pay attention*. However, one of the benefits that came when Bill went to work at Frontier Ford was he had health insurance for himself, and with a little more out of the paycheck, it covered the family. This was something very new to us in the working class because none of the jobs I had provided any benefits like health insurance, pension plan, or any of the things so important in today's world.

Our first need for the wonderful insurance was an unusual circumstance where Bill had pain in his right eye, so severe it affected his left eye as well. He went to an eye doctor who gave him medication to calm down the pain and make it so he could see, but as soon as the medication was used up, the eye acted up again. This was bad; he missed work because of it—that meant less money to pay bills.

Shelley was to be at a camp, and Bill and I were chaperones, along with other parents. Bill's medicine ran out, and by the time the camp was over, he was in more misery than usual. The eye doctor he had been seeing wasn't available (he had a drinking problem, and maybe that was why he wasn't available). At any rate, there was another eye doctor in Rapid, and I called that office. The receptionist was very rude, saying her doctor was going to be leaving early. After I pleaded, she finally gave us an appointment, saying it better be an emergency. The doctor saw Bill and immediately sent him to the hospital, saying the pain in the eye was caused by some sort of infection. The receptionist apologized. All sorts of tests were ordered, but they didn't show anything. The eye doctor then said to get ahold of a dentist to check his teeth.

I went down the list of dentists in Rapid City, trying to find one that could see him that day. We lucked out, and a Dr. Horton was just starting his practice and could get him in. He discovered four abscessed teeth. Bill's teeth never ached or bothered, but they were causing his problem. The dentist pulled two teeth in the back and drained the other two, and the eye quit hurting, and he could see again.

This remedy was short-lived, and it was decided that he would need to get all the top teeth pulled as soon as possible. Here he was, only thirty-two and going to be wearing dentures. Dr. Horton took an impression, and within a couple of days, the plate was ready. He pulled all the teeth and put the new plate in place with instructions not to remove it and, in three days, come back to the office, and he would take them out. The teeth were so natural and exactly like his original teeth. Bill and I met Bill's folks, Bea and Butch, at the Longbranch after the teeth-pulling, and Bea thought he had chickened out on getting his teeth pulled. These were the best set of teeth ever and fit like a glove.

In fact, Bill was so proud of the bite that one night, as he was sipping beer and I was with him, he stuck a straw between the molars and had me try to pull it out when he clamped down on it. I couldn't budge it. Next, he put it between his front teeth. When I pulled on the straw, out popped one of the teeth from the plate.

Oops, not a good deal. Another fellow sitting there, drinking, looked at Bill and said, "Man, you better have another beer. That thing's going to start hurting. I can see the root!"

Even after Bill took out his teeth to show him it was a plate, the guy was sure it was eventually going to hurt. Dr. Horton fixed the tooth, and we never tried that again.

I was the next one needing to see a doctor. I was twenty-nine, and I had been taking birth control pills for several years and had the same pharmacist all that time. It was time for me to see a doctor to renew the prescription, and I coaxed the pharmacist to give me another month supply. He did but then said no more until I brought in a prescription. I made the appointment begrudgingly.

The usual Pap test was performed, and I got a call that it was positive. What the heck, I didn't have time for such stuff. An appointment was set up for a DNC, and that came back with *cancer* of the uterus. The doctor called me with that news when I was at work. He had already made arrangements for a surgeon to perform the surgery. Not having any experience with such stuff, I called a nurse friend to tell her all I knew and who the surgeon was. She said he was a butcher and not to let him near me and gave me the name of a good doctor she highly recommended. I called my doctor back; he was not happy about canceling with the surgeon he had already set things in motion with. I told him I would cancel it if he wouldn't. We got it straightened out, and all went well.

My stay in the hospital was only a few days. This was in 1972, and while I was in the hospital, Bill proceeded to trade his motorcycle and got a 1972 orange Suzuki two-seater pickup. He and the girls picked me up in that little pickup, and we took a ride to Pactola Reservoir; not the best thing for someone that had just had surgery and was glued back together, but we went anyway. The girls got to ride in the bed of the pickup.

I was supposed to take it easy and rest. The worst part of being home in the daytime is you see all the dirt that is hidden in the dark of night. The rug needed cleaning, and there were other things I wanted to get done while I was home. I hired a woman that had an ad in the paper about cleaning. I should have known it wasn't going to work out to my advantage when she showed up with a little girl with her. I gave her the orders on where to start, and I took the little girl, and we went to get a rug-cleaning machine, which I had to lift to get loaded. To make a long story short, I did more work than the woman I hired. I finally paid her off for a few hours of work and did the rest myself.

Darrel Liebig was staying with us between divorcing his wife and his mother asking him to leave, and he brought with him a bunch of furniture that was in our garage. Because he hadn't paid any rent to stay with us, he agreed to sell the furniture, and we would keep the money. Another thing I should not have done, but I got some help, and we loaded the stuff and took it to a consignment auction. At least we could park in the garage again. There wasn't much money from the sale of used furniture, but it was gone.

Finally I decided I had better go back to work; at least it was a sit-down job and no heavy lifting.

The good news was back then, if you had cancer that was operable, the surgery was performed, and you were done. I always said I had a good type of cancer because once the uterus was removed, it was gone.

We didn't discuss the problem too much with the girls, and that may have been a mistake. It was quite a bit later that a teacher at teacher conferences told me that this seemed to have affected Sandra in a negative way. Sandra wouldn't talk to us about it.

THE GIRLS

As young parents go, we probably made many mistakes along the way in the way of raising our daughters. Bill's contact with them was quite minimal in the early years.

I was always eager to help them learn, read books to them daily, and worked to have them help themselves as they grew.

Shelley was very good at coloring at an early age, and when there was a coloring contest offered in the newspaper, I got the page for her to color and submitted it; she was about five at that time. It was around Easter time, and her coloring won first place. She received a *big* stuffed rabbit that was bigger than she was.

Sandra spent a good deal of her time outside with me when she was tiny. While I worked in the garden or yard, she was in her stroller or playpen. She was barely able to walk, but there was a kite-flying contest going on, and she won that as being the youngest contestant.

They learned to swim at an early age, and we belonged to the YMCA in Rapid. There was a self-defense class, and they both took that, as well as swimming lessons. In the self-defense class, there was a board-breaking demonstration, and Shelley thought that looked impressive, so she gave it a try, only to hurt the side of her hand when she hit the board, but it did break, which surprised us all. She didn't try it again, though.

There was a class in ballet, so they gave that a try for a while, but for some reason, it was short-lived. They were in Brownies and Girl Scouts for several years. Then along came 4-H, and they joined that. While in 4-H, they learned sewing, cooking, demonstrations, and even some livestock. They could join at age eight, and it was a real learning experience for us all. They made clothes in the sewing contest, had to keep record books, and in the dress review, they went shopping and purchased an entire wardrobe and then modeled it.

When we made the move to Greenbriar Street, they made friends with several of the neighbor girls. Lori Mette and Ellen Roberts were two of their close friends, both Shelley's age. Lori lived on a little farm north of our place, and they had horses. Both Lori and Ellen were in 4-H. On February 3, 1973, there was a Ground Beef Cook-off. Black Hills Power and Light Company proudly sponsored the Ground Beef Cook-off as a youth event in conjunction with the Black Hills Stock Show. Each contestant was given a pound of ground beef and had to prepare and cook it in front of the judges. We ate a lot of ground beef for about three months while Shelley and Lori worked to perfect a recipe that would please the judges, and Sandra and Ellen did the same. All that hard work paid off—Sandra and Ellen's recipe was in the semifinals, at the top of the list.

Beef and Baked Beans

1 pound ground beef
16-ounce can pork and beans in tomato sauce
1/4 cup catsup
2 tablespoons brown sugar
3 tablespoons molasses
3 tablespoons bacon bits
1/2 package dry onion soup
1 teaspoon prepared mustard
1/2 teaspoon salt
Combine the above ingredients. Break up ground beef with a fork. Stir into bean mixture. Lightly grease casserole and pour mixture in. Place cubes of sharp processed American cheese on top. Oven: 325 for 40–50 minutes.

Ellen Roberts and Sandra Sumpter, Rapid City semifinalists.

Another project the girls had was chickens. We bought the baby chicks, and they were kept in their rooms in cardboard boxes, and records were kept on feed and cost and survival. As they grew too big for the box, they went to the farm to be with the other chickens until

fair time. Because we had bought some black heavies meat-type birds, when they went to the farm, the other chickens didn't know about them and shied away from them and shunned them for quite some time.

When it was time to show them, we picked them up and brought them home with us, only to have one escape our fenced-in yard. What to do to get that bird home? I called the radio station and had them announce we were looking for a chicken and gave them a description and possible location, and pretty soon, we received a call; the lost chicken was found. It was short a few tail feathers and a little worse for the wear so not able to show it with the rest of the chickens, but at least it was alive.

The girls wanted to show horses since they loved the horses at the ranch, so we loaded two of their favorite horses up and brought them to Rapid for them to show. The first thing we learned was that you had to dress appropriately for showing horses: white shirts, cowboy hat, and black jeans. That was expensive in itself, not to mention gas to get the horses to and from the ranch. Then grooming was another issue; these horses were working horses, not glamor horses, and their tails were too long and mane unkempt. The tails, we were instructed, needed to have the hair pulled out, not just cut off blunt. Needless to say, we got through showing the horses and learned a lot in the process, but there were no blue ribbons taken there.

Sandra tested out playing in the school band and was given a cello to learn to play. It was big and hard to handle, so she used a wagon to tote it back and forth from school to home. It was difficult for her to learn, so she dropped that.

She had another friend that lived up the street from us, Lorna Squire, and they were in the same grade.

Pictured: Sandra, Lori, Ellen, and Shelley

The girls and their friends helped us with mowing the lawn and cleaning up the backyard, where the dogs always were.

When we cut the grass, it was loaded in the little pickup and taken to Lori's to feed the horses. We had a riding mower at the Greenbriar home, but it had a bit of steering problem: if you turned the wheel too far one way or the other, something messed up, and the steering became the opposite of what it should be; thus if you turned left, the mower went right and vice versa. One time, with Ellen at the wheel, that happened, and she was out in the busy street before she could correct the situation. Luckily the traffic was light that day!

Little pickup used for the grass clippings

We had the luxury of having a boat, and Bill was really good and patient at teaching folks to water-ski. He could get even the most unbalanced folks up and going. We spent some great summer months on weekends water-skiing.

The girls were getting older and more capable of taking care of themselves after school, but we still felt they needed some supervision, so we took in a girl that was attending trade school to be a supervisor after school. Sue Berdick was one such young lady that lived with us for a while. She worked across the street at the Baptist Church nursery so was close at hand if she was needed. She would take care of the animals if we were gone to the ranch, and went with us to the lake and learned to water-ski. We were fortunate to have such a great gal. When she graduated, we tried out another gal, and that didn't work out at all. She brought boyfriends into the house, didn't help with the girls and in general; it was a short relationship. After that experience, we pretty much left the girls to take care of themselves with instructions. I was just a phone call away, too, so that helped.

Once, Sandra called and asked if she could take her buggy outside. I said I didn't see any reason why not, but she whispered into the phone that I was to tell her no because she didn't want to and had called so I could tell her no, and she could tell her friends that "her mom said no." I followed her lead and said *no*.

CHARLIE

How many of you ever thought it would be fun to have a monkey? Raise your hand. Can you see my hand in the air? When I was growing up, in the comic books, there always was an ad for a squirrel monkey, would fit in your pocket, and would make a great pet. I thought that would be fun to get. However, being in the country, I already had cats, chickens, sheep, calves, horses, and the family working dog, so the thought of having a monkey was pushed aside.

Fast forward to having two girls of our own. Shelley wanted to get a monkey and was saving her money specifically for buying one. That inner child in me sure didn't discourage it. In fact, every so often, we would stop by the pet shop and check out the animals for sale. Usually there were kittens, puppies, fish, hamsters, and even mice, but no monkeys.

One fateful day, as we were running errands, we decided to check out the pet shop again. Much to our surprise, the owner had several monkeys, a couple of squirrel monkeys in small cages, and a capuchin monkey in a bigger cage. Oh, were they cute. The squirrel monkeys had a price tag of $40, then the small cage was also $40. On her last check, Shelley only had a total of $40 saved, and she told the shop owner that. We were defeated so decided to just enjoy our time while there, looking at all the animals. The capuchin monkey was a busy little fellow and would try to pick your pocket if you got too close to his cage. He chittered at the girls and would even take their finger through the wire cage. The price tag on that fellow was $80, then the addition of a cage would add up to way more than Shelley had.

After browsing through the store and playing a little more with the capuchin monkey, the store owner came over with a proposal. He was willing to sell that monkey and throw in a cage for $40. What? We couldn't believe our ears, but Shelley quickly agreed to take him, but we had to run home to get the money. It didn't take us very long before we were back at the pet store. The owner met us at the door, rather red-faced, with the monkey in a smaller cage, put monkey and cage in our little pickup, grabbed the money, and the deal was done. This transaction should have given us a clue as to what we were getting ourselves into, but we were naive and gullible.

This little fellow was named Charlie. He was black with a brown face that wrinkled like a little old man and had beautiful brown eyes. We set the cage in the living room and proceeded to get to know Charlie. Bill was in his swim trunks after his shower and was lying on the couch. Charlie turned on all his monkey charm, looking at Bill with those pleading brown eyes and chittering at him.

Bill said, "Let him out. He can't hurt anything!" Those were famous last words. I went to the kitchen and put a cover on the butter dish on the table and told the girls they could let him out.

Once that little door to his cage was opened, Charlie shot out of it and was on the run through the house. He hit the kitchen table in an instant and grabbed the butter dish with his tail and headed for the curtains in the living room. Up them, he went at full speed, losing the top off the butter dish and flinging butter all around.

From his perch on top of the curtains, he spotted Bill's hairy chest, and down he came and jumped in the middle of Bill and started chittering to his chest and rubbing his little hands through the hair.

We had no idea how old Charlie was, but he must have been quite young. Any attempt to hold him or grab him sent him flying to another part of the house or up the curtains again. What were we to do? It was getting late and bedtime. Finally in desperation, when he ran into Shelley's room, we shut the door, and as the lights went off for the night, and I checked in to see how Shelley was doing with her monkey, Charlie was sitting by her head, and she was fast asleep.

We needed a quick course on the care and feeding of a monkey, and fast. We found a little book that told about how to care for a monkey. Charlie was the type of monkey that organ grinders used to use, where when they played music, the monkey would go through the crowd with a cup, and people would drop money it in. We had the feeling that if Charlie was that monkey, and a person didn't put money in the cup, he would jump them for it.

First we needed to have some sort of control if we wanted to take Charlie out of his cage. We got a tiny little collar and put it on. It took him about ten seconds to pull it off his head and be on the loose. Next, we got a sort of figure-eight collar, and that worked. Now the girls could take him out and had some control.

The little cage he was in had a sort of litter tray in the bottom, so it could be cleaned since he was like a bird as far as going to the bathroom. Covering the litter tray was a grill-type cover. Well, our little Houdini was no dummy, and probably the pet store owner found that out. He reached through the grill cover and pushed the litter tray out from the bottom of the cage, then he held himself up by the tail and pushed the grill out the bottom of the cage. Now he was on the floor, and with those two little monkey hands, he lifted the rest of the cage and was *free*! We had the only house that could self-destruct in an hour if Charlie was on the loose. After seeing how he had pulled his escape, I wired the grill in place.

Maybe the $40 Shelley spent was something we could reimburse her for out of our own pocket and find a new home for Charlie. He was about too smart for us.

Well, we weren't going to give up that easy. We had learned what he liked in food and actually found monkey chow at the local feedstore, as well as fruit treats. The book said that monkeys like alcohol and would sometimes fake a sneeze in order to get a little whiskey. Well, we didn't have any whiskey around, but there was beer, and he did like that.

Much like a child, Charlie needed to be disciplined. One time, when he was on the leash, he came over and bit my finger. That wasn't going to go unchecked. I reeled him to me and swatted him on the behind; he grabbed his head and threw himself back on the couch, then rushed over and lightly bit my finger again. Again, reeled him to me and swatted him, and back he fell to the couch, holding his head. The third time, he came to me and took my finger in his little hands and proceeded to chitter at it and lick it. He never bit me again.

We had a kitten, and Charlie would pet the kitten through the wire cage as it sat beside it. The girls thought it would be nice to let Charlie hold the kitten, so they put it inside the cage. Charlie sat on his bar and tried his best to not look at the kitten and totally ignore it. When the girls opened the door to take the kitten out, Charlie pushed it out, too.

Charlie fell in love with Bill. Bill and some of his friends welded together a much-bigger cage using chain-link fence on it all around; it was a sturdy built cage, and big. I wonder how we ever got that heavy thing down the basement. In the evening, when Charlie heard Bill coming home, he would get as close to the front of the cage and chitter to him to come and see him. When Bill took a shower, he took Charlie in with him and soaped him up, and Charlie loved that. I would wait outside the shower and towel him down, while Bill finished his shower. Charlie was dirty from food and such, and as I said, he wasn't toilet trained.

One of Bill's friends stopped by one evening for a visit. Charlie was outside the cage and came over to meet this new person. The guy had a tattoo of a scantily dressed girl on his forearm. Charlie could see this image through the hair on his arm and proceeded to try to bite away the hair. The fellow took out a sharp knife from his pocket and proceeded to shave away the hair. Charlie spent the rest of the visit cradling his arm and talking to the tattoo.

The weakest link! Charlie was strong for his little stature. That awesome cage that was built special for him had a few weakest links. The first discovery was that Charlie figured out how to reach around through the chain links and remove the bolt that was holding the door closed. Freedom at last, now he had two floors he could tear up—the basement and the upstairs. We put a clip-type latch, and that worked. However, Charlie tested all the welds on the fence and found another weakest link. He was able to break through the weld and had enough room to squeeze out. Could we ever outsmart him?

The time he opened his door, we were at the ranch for the weekend and had given him enough food and water to hold him. He had the whole weekend to tear up things, and he was a busy little guy. When we got home, what a sight! The curtains in the living room were hanging half off and half on. Plants were uprooted and soil all over; he had turned on the burners on the stove, knocked things out of the cupboards that landed on the hot stove, which set off the smoke alarms we had. How he did it, we will never know, but the things on the stove were in the sink, and the burners were turned off. The smoke alarm that was going off, he had gotten it off its hanger above the basement door, and it was on the floor. He had taken brads and mixed them through a hundred-pound bag of sugar we had brought back when we were in Mexico, and the trail of destruction he left behind was staggering. When he heard us open the back door, he ran to his cage, grabbed the door, and pulled it shut behind him. Then wrapping his tail around the fencing in the cage and bracing with his back legs and holding on with his hands, he chittered in a pleading voice to not hurt him. What a cleanup we had.

One night, Bill was out grilling hamburgers with the fellows and had put a six-pack of beer on the air conditioner in the front of the house, and he had Charlie outside unsupervised with no leash. Pretty soon, a neighbor came walking up to the house with Charlie on his shoulder. He said, "Charlie's been drinking and causing a problem." He had opened all the cans of beer and drank and spilled them as he drank, then he took off down the street and was in the neighbor's car turning on the lights, honking the horn, and generally having a good time.

Another time, Charlie was on my shoulder when the pastor and a lady from church stopped for a visit. When I opened the door and invited them in, Charlie decided to go and check out these people and jumped from my shoulder to the shoulder of the visiting lady. She was not impressed, and that visit was very short.

Shelley took him to school for show-and-tell. She was in middle school, and Charlie was a big hit. I went and picked him up and took him home after her introduction for show-and-tell. The principal was so impressed with Charlie he staged a whole program around Charlie

Is Coming, and it had quite a buildup and drew a big attendance at a program put on by the middle school kids.

The antics of Charlie could fill an entire book. One time, we were going on vacation to Arkansas. What to do with Charlie? We shopped around and found a pet store that agreed to keep him. We warned them about his ability to do things. When we went to pick him up, we found out he had gotten into a lot of mischief.

The first night in their care, he had opened his cage, then proceeded to open all the other cages and let every animal in the place out. He got into the food, and when the owners and their daughter arrived to the mess, he grabbed the little girl's glasses. After all that, they still loved Charlie; in fact, so much so that they got their own capuchin monkey and built a big cage with a tree in it for its habitat.

It was much safer for us all if Charlie accompanied us when we went to the ranch. Here he is perched on Bill's shoulder at Lake Waggoner. Our pictures of Charlie are few and far between, mostly because he was just too fast for us, I guess. One time, he slipped away from us when we were at the ranch and couldn't be found in the Quonset he was hiding in. We shut the doors and had to be back to Rapid for work. We told Dad not to shoot him, but we would be back to get him next weekend. All the while Charlie was confined to the Quonset, he disassembled two sprayers and managed to find all sorts of things to occupy his time. Once while at the ranch, he escaped among the combines and wouldn't come to us, just kept hiding. He got in one of their trucks and got out the manual, and it seemed he was reading it and would tear out the pages as he got done, broke sunglasses, and took the keys and lost them. He was a busy little fellow.

Once, the girls loaded up their dogs in the back of the little orange pickup, and Charlie was in the front, on my lap, thinking he was driving, and a lady friend was along, and we went for a drive in downtown Rapid to go to the A&W for root beer floats. We had a lot of lookers at this strange group.

FLOOD

Our usual Friday night entertainment was to attend the car races. Bill liked to hang out around the drivers and pit crews and, on occasion, helped them with mechanical things. These races were run on a lot of beer before, during, and after the race by all participants. I wasn't a great fan of all the drinking, and many of the women and girls that hung around the cars also drank a lot and were known to sleep around with the fellows. Another thing that didn't endear me to the car races.

One time, when there was another racetrack down by Hermosa, we were in attendance; and for some reason, I got peeved at Bill. I think I thought we were going out because I had on a dress but then was really disappointed to find out our date was a racetrack. During these races, they had Powder Puff races, where the ladies would drive. Some of them were darned good drivers and had done it quite a bit. When they announced they needed drivers for the Powder Puff races, I stomped down to the pits and asked a friend if I could drive. Well, they stuck me—dress and all—into that car, which was always last in the heat races, and off I went with the rest of the pack. Bill was glad the announcer didn't get the last name right when he was announcing the drivers. What an experience. I came in last; the turns were hard to see because the lights were poor, but anyway I got over my mad.

We were at the racetrack in the valley, Black Hills Speedway, the night of June 9, 1972, a Friday night. It was sprinkling a little, and the races were on hold. We listened to the radio, and the announcer said there was a flash flood warning for Rapid City. How could this little bit of rain cause a flash flood? Eventually the races were called off. Generally Bill liked to go to a little bar just off West Omaha but that night decided to go home. We still had Rich Cordwell and Dick Reoh living with us. We went to bed that night, not knowing what transpired as we slept.

When we got up the next morning, there was an eerie silence in the air. We had no electricity, and it was foggy out. Both Rich and Dick were in the house, and they told us about their night. Dick heard that flooding was going to happen, so he went to his sister's place in West Rapid and helped them sandbag around their place. Rich somehow ended up in a boat helping rescue folks from a trailer park on the east of Rapid. There was nothing left of a lot of homes along Rapid Creek that ran along Omaha Street. That little bar I mentioned was nothing but a cement slab. We got in the car and tried to go east from our house, only to find the street flooded. We went down Haines Avenue, toward Omaha Street, and could see the devastation before our eyes. The town was in shambles. Rescue crews had worked through the night and were still at it that morning.

The water had receded as quick as it came, leaving behind death and destruction. We learned as the days wore on that 238 human lives were lost, 3,000 injured, 720 homes destroyed, and another 1,400 homes were severely damaged. Help was needed everywhere. Bill volunteered to man a Caterpillar at the dump. The cleanup went on for weeks. One man working at the dump quit because when the truck unloaded its load, a dead person surfaced.

Prior to the flood, the Mechanics Union had declared a strike, and Bill and all of the personnel at Frontier Ford and all the other car mechanics and workers were on strike. Bill didn't agree with the union but had to carry a picket sign. The flood broke up that picket, and the union was voted out. The bosses were good people and didn't deserve being picketed because the union decided that is what would be done.

The flood had stacked cars on top of each other inside the Ford building, as well as outside. Over five thousand vehicles were ruined. Bill's toolbox was full of mud and water.

I joined another friend, and we fixed food for workers. Anybody that had a stove that wasn't electric was working to help those that were picking up the pieces after the flood. We had a bad experience with a service station. Loretta was driving her car, and the Safeway store had power and was open on St. Patrick Street. We went there with our children along to stock up on more food, and as we pulled into the store, one of the tires was going flat. We pulled around to this service station that was right on the corner, and there were several men there, but they refused to fix the tire and demanded we get it off their property. Loretta got groceries, and she and the children walked the five blocks to her house. The car was unfamiliar to her, and we couldn't find the jack. I waited with the car, and the men at the service station yelled at me, ran a car toward this car parked on the street, and in general were trying to scare me. I finally found someone that could help change the tire and got it out of there. After the cleanup was done, I wrote the main company a letter, and that person was put out of business.

Bill worked at the dump but had to quit after about a week because he came down with bacterial pneumonia.

On Monday morning, I reported to work at the law office for Ramon Roubideaux. When he came in, I asked him why we were there. We closed the office, and he went and helped direct traffic, and I went to the radio station to help compile a list of those missing people and hopefully check off those found safe.

Less than a month before the flood, we had sold the house on Fairmont Boulevard. It remained high and dry, as did our house on Greenbriar. Had we still owned that little house, it would have sold for double what we got for it because houses were in high demand and short supply.

I cannot begin to tell you enough about this terrible flood. It still ranks among the deadliest and most destructive in US history. Some folks blamed cloud seeding that had taken place in the weeks before it happened. We were in a drought at the time. Changes were made along Rapid Creek, and development was limited for many years to avoid such a disaster in the future.

AND THE WINNER IS

After I became eligible to belong to the NSA (National Secretaries Association), I joined the Mount Rushmore Chapter. Because there was no such thing as a provisional member, and I had to gain work experience to belong, it wasn't until 1968 that I became a regular member. I was very active in the chapter projects. We hosted fashion shows to promote stores and businesses, sold television ads to raise funds, and were very busy. I held the office of corresponding secretary several years. I served on all committees and acted as chairman of many of these committees. I served as division FSA (Future Secretaries Association) and was very active with the FSA chapters in Rapid City, mentoring the upcoming secretaries.

It was in May of 1974, I was honored to be named Secretary of the Year for outstanding service to the secretarial profession, Mount Rushmore Chapter.

I was a SOTY contestant at the division meeting in Aberdeen. What a truly great honor, and it was all made possible because Mr. Frieberg thought I should be connected with other working secretaries.

Here I am, fueling up the camper for the trip to Aberdeen.

My support group that rode all the way to Aberdeen with me. L to R: Alice Farrington, Marsha Sumpter, Dianne Stratton, JoAnn Hoar holding flowers, and Marilyn Simpson. May 18, 1974.

The camper was one Bill and I spotted at Frontier Ford, it looking like a circus but had all the comforts needed. A home built on a Ford truck chassis. Our family had many fun adventures in it as well as our group that went to the SOTY event.

HELP

The need for help on a farm/ranch is continual. So often the help is homegrown, meaning there are children that grow up to be the workforce, and when they become adults, it is the hope that at least one will make this lifestyle their chosen occupation.

It isn't an easy occupation. You battle Mother Nature at every turn of the calendar. You gamble with your life savings daily. There are few holidays; usually you are dirt poor and short of money continually. You get to know the banker up front and personal, as you need to borrow money just to keep going some years. There is no disability, workman's comp, or any of the other securities so many jobs offer. If you want those things, you have to pay for them yourself.

Health insurance is something else. If you are young and healthy, it may be an expense you forgo. If you owe the bank a lot of money, they make you be insured.

Mom and Dad were getting along in age and needing more help. The part-time helpers that Dad hired to help farm were not ones that wanted to help with cattle and sheep. Young neighbor men were getting established on their own and unable to devote full-time to being hired men for anybody.

Dick Reoh, who was living with us, was unemployed, and we visited with him about going down to work for the folks. He would get room and board and wages. It sounded pretty good, so off he went to become a farmer or rancher.

This arrangement didn't last very long before he was back in Rapid. It was more work than he planned, long hours, and the pay was figured on a monthly basis, not hourly.

The corporation Fairchild Enterprises Inc., established in 1970, was totally funded by Mom and Dad putting all the acres of the place into shares and assigning them a value. These shares were assigned to the three officers: Wayne Fairchild, president; Marsha Sumpter, vice president; and Ruth Fairchild, secretary-treasurer. Now everything was done under the corporation umbrella.

They were still needing to come up with some steady reliable help or were seriously considering selling off the whole place.

In 1971, the farming paid off big-time; it was like hitting the mother lode of wheat.

This picture shows Dad standing in the wheat pile just to the south of the main house. Although it's hard to define the wheat pile from the sky, there are one hundred thousand bushels of wheat that Dad is standing in. This crop was phenomenal; it cleared away all debt and allowed for payment on dividends to each of the shareholders—Wayne, Ruth, Kent, Bruce, and Marsha. Each of us kids were so thankful for the added revenue and, of course, promptly spent the money. Bill wanted a boat, and we added that to our fun things and managed to take the girls and their friends water-skiing most every weekend during the summer.

This still did not solve the problem of help at the farm/ranch. Kent and his family were well established in his navy career. Bruce and his family were settled in Bothell, Washington, with both him and Lois having full-time jobs. Bill and I also were settled in Rapid City with full-time jobs. However, Kent and Bruce had tried coming back to the farm, and it didn't work. Who will save the family farm?

Finally at a special meeting of shareholders held in San Diego, California, with all shareholders present, the minutes read:

> *The purpose the meeting was to approve the up-grading of the farm buildings and secure hired help.*
>
> *Upon motion duly made, seconded and carried, it was unanimously voted that the corporation shall forthwith attempt to secure full-time hired help and in so doing, also construct a new home at the farm headquarters for the use of the hired help or manager. It was also agreed that Bill Sumpter be hired as the full-time hired help and reside at the farm headquarters and that no rent be paid for the home used by the hired help, or if the Internal Revenue Service insisted that rent be paid, that any rent collected be in the least possible amount necessary.*
>
> *Upon motion duly made, seconded, and carried, it was unanimously voted that the corporation reimburse each shareholder for expenses of travel to the corporate meeting in the amount of $140.00 each to Bruce Fairchild and Marsha M. Sumpter and for food and lodging in the amount of $140.00 to Kent Fairchild. The treasurer was instructed to make payment of the same.*
>
> *Upon motion duly made, seconded and carried, it was unanimously voted that the corporation shall forthwith up-grade all buildings on the farm headquarters and replace the existing shop building with a new structure and erect a new grain Quonset, and repair and rebuild such other buildings as the manager sees fit.*

Were Bill and I and our girls going to be able to save the family farm?

www.ingramcontent.com/pod-product-compliance
Lightning Source LLC
Chambersburg PA
CBHW051218120626
46547CB00013B/1401